KOMODO CERAMIC CHARCOAL GRILL COOKBOOK 1000

1000 DAYS YUMMY, RELAX RECIPES AND TECHNIQUES
FOR THE WORLD'S BEST BARBECUE

ROSS ROBBINS

Copyright © 2021 by Ross Robbins - All rights reserved.

The content contained within this book may not be reproduced, duplicated, or transmitted without direct written permission from the author or the publisher. Under no circumstances will any blame or legal responsibility be held against the publisher, or author, for any damages, reparation, or monetary loss due to the information contained within this book, either directly or indirectly.

Legal Notice: This book is copyright protected. It is only for personal use. You cannot amend, distribute, sell, use, quote or paraphrase any part, or the content within this book, without the consent of the author or publisher.

Disclaimer Notice: Please note the information contained within this document is for educational and entertainment purposes only. All effort has been executed to present accurate, up to date, reliable, complete information. No warranties of any kind are declared or implied. Readers acknowledge that the author is not engaged in the rendering of legal, financial, medical, or professional advice. The content within this book has been derived from various sources. Please consult a licensed professional before attempting any techniques outlined in this book. By reading this document, the reader agrees that under no circumstances is the author responsible for any losses, direct or indirect, that are incurred as a result of the use of the information contained within this document, including, but not limited to, errors, omissions, or inaccuracies.

CONTENTS

INTRODUCTION 8
    How Does A Kamado Grill Work? 8
    The Benefits of the Komodo Kamado Grill 8
    How to Use Your Komodo Kamado Grill 10
    How to Deeply Clean Your Komodo Kamado Grill 12

FISH AND SEAFOOD 13
    Big Game Recipes 13
    Arctic Char With Blood Orange Salad 14
    Grilled Lobster 14
    Clam Bake 15
    Creole Bbq Shrimp 16
    Smoked Planked Trout 17
    Grilled Shrimp Cocktail With Fire-roasted Cocktail Sauce 18
    Grilled Oysters 19
    Grilled Tuna Sandwiches With Chipotle Mayo 19
    Grilled Calamari Salad With Lemon Caper Vinaigrette 20
    Seafood & Smoked Gouda Pasta 21
    Roasted Halibut With Greek Relish 22
    Festive Kabobs 22
    Oysters On The Half Shell 23
    Tuna Artichoke Melt 23
    Grilled Lobster Tails With Smoked Caper Cream 24
    Paella On The Egg 25
    Lemon Bed Cod 26
    Southwest Baked Oysters 26
    Bourbon-glazed Cold Smoked Salmon 27
    Mediterranean Surf And Turf Kabobs 28
    Seared Ahi Tuna 29
    Cedar Planked Salmon With Honey Glaze 29
    Cold-smoked Rock Shrimp 30
    Grilled Oysters With Garlic Butter 31

POULTRY 32
    Smoked Spanish Chicken 32
    Hatch Chile Salsa And Chicken Casserole 33

Butter-injected Turkey And Sides 34
Beer Can Chicken 35
Garfunkel Chicken 35
Rotisserie Style Chicken 36
Bacon Wrapped Jalapeño Stuffed Chicken Thighs 36
Chicken Keema Burgers 37
Grilled Hot Candy Chicken Wings 38
Smokey Thai Pulled Chicken Sandwiches 39
Chicken & Veggie Stir-fry 41
Chimichurri Smoked Chicken Salad Sandwich 42
Grilled Vidalia Onion Chicken Peach Skewers 43
Rotisserie Chicken 44
Barbecue Chicken With Alabama White Sauce 45
Caribbean Chicken Thigh Kebabs 46
Smoky Thai Pulled Chicken Sandwiches 47
Cuban Chicken Bombs 49
Thai Stuffed Chicken Drumsticks 50
Country Chicken Saltimbocca 51
Brined Roasted Turkey 52
Spicy Bourbon Barrel Bbq Wings 53
Peking Duck 54
Smoked Turkey 55
Smoked Curried Chicken Salad With Grilled Naan Bread 56

DESSERTS 57
Orange Scented Vanilla Cake 57
Sourdough Baguette 58
3 Ingredient Fruit Cobbler 59
Almond Cream Cake 60
Buttermilk Biscuits 61
Fresh Peach Crisp 61
Grilled Naan 62
Grilled Pineapple Sundaes 62
4 Ingredient, No Knead Bread 63
Seasonal Fruit Cobbler 64
Nutella And Strawberry Pizza 65
S'mores Pizza 65
Chocolate Cake 66
Bread Pudding 67

- Grilled Sopapillas 67
- Lemon Poppy Seed Cake 68
- Banana Boats 68
- Peach Dutch Baby 69
- Berry Upside-down Cake 70
- Apple Cake 71
- Grilled Fruit Pie 72
- Death By Chocolate 73
- Chocolate Chip Cookie Peanut Butter Cup S'mores 73
- Best Banana Bread 74
- Peaches And Pound Cake 74

BEEF 75
- Grilled Veal Chop With Fresh Herbs 75
- Italian Sausage Sliders 75
- Butter-rubbed Lamb Chops With Fig Mustard Aioli 76
- Stir-fry Szechuan Beef 77
- Rack Of Lamb 77
- Smoked Brisket Roll 78
- Dad's Grilled Steak 79
- Grilled Entrecôte Of Beef 80
- Steak Roll-ups With Porcini Mushroom Rub 81
- Steak With Caramelized Onions 82
- Bacon Cheeseburger Hotdogs 83
- Dr. Bbq's Smoked Flat-cut Brisket With Coffee 84
- Smoked Beef Ribs With Mustard Marinade 85
- Rouladen 86
- Holiday Sirloin Roast 86
- Beef Asparagus Stir Fry 87
- Chris Lane's Rib-eye Steaks On The Egg 87
- Italian Meatballs 88
- Smoked & Braised Beef Chuck Steak 89
- Smoked Goat Bolognese 90
- Grilled Cheesesteak Pizza 91
- Antelope Medallions 92
- Smoked Oxtail Stew 93
- Wild Mushroom And Blue Cheese Stuffed Burger 94
- Jim Beam Hamburgers 94

BURGERS 95

Breakfast Burger 95
Classic American Burger 96
Oahu Burger 96
Quesadilla Burger 97
The Crowned Jewels Burger 98
"the Masterpiece" 99

PORK 100

Bbq Chicken Quarters 100
Pork Belly Burnt Ends 101
Pulled Pork Baked Beans 101
Sunday Dinner Pork Roast 102
Cherry-smoked Turkey Legs 103
Double Smoked Maple Bourbon Glazed Ham 104
Dill Pickle Injected Chicken Bog 105
Chile Rubbed Grilled Pork Chops 106
Pulled Pork Sandwiches 107
Slow Roasted Pork Belly 108
Stir-fried Cucumber And Pork With Golden Garlic 109
Pork Curry 110
Charlotte Pork Chops 111
Pulled Pork Nachos With Fire-roasted Salsa 112
Smoked Spicy Korean Spare Ribs 113
Whole Roasted Chicken With Garlic & Fresh Herb Butter 114
Duck & Potatoes 115
Potato Salad With Bacon 116
Spanish Pork Tenderloins 117
Smoked Spareribs 118
Twice-smoked Ham 119
Barbecue Pork Shoulder 120
Turkey Bacon Dogs 120
Dr. Bbq's Spare Rib Surprise 121
Dutch Oven Pork Roast 122

SIDES 123

Alligator Eggs 123
Wood-plank Loaded Mashed Potatoes 124
Grilled Watermelon Salad 125
Grilled Onions 125
Grilled Sweet Potatoes 126

Grilled Lemon Garlic Zucchini	126
Wood-plank Stuffed Tomatoes	127
Parmesan Zucchini Spears	127
Soba Noodle Bowl	128
Dutch Oven Black Beans	129
Bacon Wrapped Pineapple	129
Corn, Bacon & Chorizo Hash	130
Grilled Polenta	131
Mac And Cheese	132
Breakfast Casserole	132
Corn & Poblano Pudding	133
Grilled Endive Salad	134
Roasted Potatoes	135
Burnt End Baked Beans	135

INTRODUCTION

How Does A Kamado Grill Work?

A kamado is no ordinary barbecue. Its strength lies partly in the combination of the oval shape and the possibility to regulate the air flow. Ceramic kamados also have the advantage of the material, which insulates and reflects heat.

You need to close the lid during cooking. This has to be done after each action and with every cooking technique. As soon as the lid is closed, the shape of the kamado creates a current of hot air. Because only some of the air can escape, the heat circulates around the ingredient or dish, a bit like a charcoal-fired convection oven. By closing the lid, you make sure that as little heat as possible is lost and that the ceramic barbecue maintains the desired temperature. This gives you good control over the cooking process.

The Benefits of the Komodo Kamado Grill

There are several ways Kamado Grills can benefit the backyard griller who is looking to enhance their outdoor cooking experience:

1. Versatility

Kamado Grills are exceptional for grilling, smoking, baking, BBQ, and roasting. This versatility allows the outdoor cook many unique options in one grill.

Feel like making a true wood fired pizza ? Because of its design, kamado grills make exceptional pizza ovens since they are extremely efficient at insulating and circulating heat throughout the grill. This results in a crispy bottom crust while perfectly melting the top layer of cheese.

And don't forget about the classics either. Steaks, ribs, burgers, the Kamado can cook them all with that classic lump charcoal flavor.

2. Flavor

Kamado Grills use wood lump charcoal which results in a tasty smoke and charcoal flavor that is classically associated with grilling.

Ceramic charcoal grills also do a tremendous job at retaining the moisture of whatever you are cooking. Since air is locked tightly, your meat remains more tender and juicier than it would on a regular charcoal grill.

3. Steady Temperatures

Since Kamado Grills are so well insulated, temperatures hold relatively steady for longer periods of time compared to a traditional charcoal grill. There is a learning curve to controlling temperatures as you will need to play around with the dampers to balance the intake and outflow of air.

In short: More air = more heat, less air = less heat.

4. Longevity

As champion Pit Master Chris Lilly states quite perfectly

"Ask your children what color they want, because they will inherit it."

As long as you treat your Kamado with care (and don't drop it from a height where it can crack), it should last a very long time.

5. Maintenance is Simple

Cleaning and maintaining a Kamado Grill is a breeze. Simply clean your grates and gently brush out the bottom. The ceramic is self-cleaning so do not use a wire brush as they can damage the surface.

6. A Great Grill for the Winter

Because Kamados are constructed to have such effective insulation, cold temperatures do not have the same effect on internal temperatures as it does on other grills. You may have to use more fuel to bring your grill up to its desired temperature, but once it reaches that temp, it will hold much better than a standard charcoal or propane grill.

How to Use Your Komodo Kamado Grill

1. Looftlighter or Electric Starter

Perhaps the easiest way to light your charcoal is with a powered heat source.

Electric starters have been around for decades, and they're simple to operate. Using an electric heating element not unlike what you'll find on a stovetop to ignite the coals, you just plug it in, turn it on, and wait.

A Looftlighter is, essentially, the world's most intense blow dryer. It employs super-heated air and a powerful fan to heat charcoal until it fires up. Not going to lie – they're pretty cool.

2. Pyramid Method

This is a classic strategy used in standard charcoal grills. All you have to do is pile your charcoal in a pyramid shape and insert two or three fire starters. Just light the fire starters, and soon they will fire up the charcoal.

With a regular grill, you'd want to spread your charcoal around, but since we want a pyramid shape anyway, there's no need to touch anything after lighting.

3. Chimney Starter

If you have a traditional charcoal grill, there's a pretty good chance you already own a chimney starter. If you don't here's a quick synopsis of how they work:

A chimney starter is a cylinder of metal with a handle on one side, and a grate about three-quarters of the way down on the inside. You fill the large side of the cylinder with charcoal and stuff the small, bottom section with newspaper and set the whole thing down on a fireproof surface.

Light up the paper, and before long, the charcoal will catch. Once it's nicely smoldering, carefully pour the coals into your firebox and arrange.

Of the three methods, we most recommend using a Looftlighter or fire starters. While chimneys are great, it can be awkward to pour the lit coals into your Kamado and then arrange them properly.

4. A Word on Lighting Fluids

If you and charcoal grilling go way back, there's a good chance you've used lighting fluids. Time was, it was pretty much standard practice for cookouts.

Simply squirt a flammable liquid on your briquettes, and light it up. As the fluid burned off, it set the briquettes to smoldering.

Yes, it works like a charm. It's also a bit dangerous if you're not careful.

The biggest problem, however, is it can add a nasty chemical taste to your food. You didn't just shell out big bucks for a kamado to eat brisket with an aftertaste of kerosene, now did you?

In a standard grill, you can get away with using an accelerant, then letting the coals rip until every single one is burning and ashed over. At this point, you can be sure all accelerant has burned away.

With many cooking techniques in a kamado, however, you only have a small portion of charcoal lit, and close down the vents to keep a lower temperature. The fire then spreads coal to coal over many hours, allowing a very long, low n slow cook.

This means, however, that any accelerant used will not have burned off and will be present to taint the flavor of your food.

So our recommendation: **NEVER** use lighting fluids in a Kamado cooker.

5. Flip Your Lid and Open Your Vents

As we've said, you need oxygen for the fire to burn. Controlling the flow of air into and out of your Kamado is the key to adjusting the temperature.

For now, though, open the bottom vent all the way and leave the lid open to get your charcoal burning.

After about 10 minutes, close the lid, but fully open the top vent. In general, you should start closing your vents when you're about 50F (28C) below your target, but we'll have more specific instructions on this later.

How to Deeply Clean Your Komodo Kamado Grill

So the time has come to get stuck into a deep clean on your kamado grill.

For all the regular ash removal and mold cleaning you do, it's still important to do a deep clean on your kamado every few months.

Don't worry though. This is a lot more straightforward than you might think, and can easily be broken down into just a few steps.

1. Place all components such as cooking grates and deflector plates in their allotted place in the grill.
2. Heat up the grill with the lid closed and air vents/dampers wide open. Aim for about 500-600°F.
3. Allow the grill to stay at this temperature for about 30 minutes, before then closing the vents and allow the grill to cool down.
4. Once the grill has cooled, open the lid and remove the grill grates and deflector plates. The long exposure to the heat will have burned away much of the dirt and grease, but you will then have to use a grill brush to clean away the rest. Don't use any soap, water or chemicals for this.
5. Remove any coal inside the kamado, and then take out any other components in the grill.
6. Remove any residual ash. This can most efficiently be done with a vacuum clean. Follow this up by using a slightly damp cloth or paper towel to pick up any stubborn ash.
7. Remove the ash tray and empty it.
8. Put all components back in the grill, and place lid back on grill.

And that's it. It's a lot easier than people think, and only needs to be done once or twice a year. In comparison to regular charcoal or gas grills, kamado grills are far easier to clean and lower maintenance.

FISH AND SEAFOOD

Big Game Recipes

Servings: 12
Cooking Time: 70 Minutes

Ingredients:

- 1 tablespoon ancho chile powder
- 1 ½ tablespoons onion powder
- 1 ½ tablespoons garlic powder
- 1 tablespoon thyme, dried
- 1 tablespoon black pepper
- ½ teaspoon cinnamon
- 1 tablespoon all-spice
- 1 tablespoon smoked paprika
- ½ teaspoon nutmeg
- 1 each Falconer's Flight hops pellet
- 1 cup sugar
- ½ cup blood orange juice
- ½ cup chicken stock
- 1 pound chicken wings
- 1 cup Dirty Bird Seasoning
- 1 cup clams, chopped
- 3 cups clam juice
- 2 tablespoons butter
- 9 pieces Tater Tots
- 3 pieces bacon
- 1 cup celery, diced small
- 3 cups heavy cream
- 1 cup pearl onions
- Tabasco to taste
- 2 tablespoons all-purpose flour
- 1 bay leaf
- 1 teaspoon thyme, chopped
- Salt to taste
- Pepper to taste

Directions:

1. Combine all ingredients in a bowl until uniformly mixed. Reserve.
2. In saucepot, add all ingredients. Allow to simmer approximately 10 minutes or until the sugar dissolves. Remove the hops pellet. Reserve.
3. Preheat the grill to 350°F using direct heat with a cast iron grate installed.
4. In a bowl, combine Dirty Bird Seasoning and chicken wings until the wings are uniformly coated.
5. Place seasoned chicken wings on the kamado grill and cook for approximately 20, or until an internal temperature of 165°F is achieved. Turn wings to ensure even cooking.
6. Toss cooked chicken wings in the Blood Orange Gastrique and serve hot.
7. Cut bacon into thirds. Wrap around each individual Tater Tot. Place on a perforated baking sheet and bake for 20 minutes or until bacon is crispy. Next preheat cast iron skillet on your grill.
8. Once hot add butter, then saute onions and celery until tender and slightly translucent. Coat cooked vegetables with all-purpose flour then deglaze with clam juice.
9. Next add clams, heavy cream, tabasco, bay leaf, thyme, salt, and pepper. Allow to simmer for 30 minutes.
10. Add bacon wrapped tater tots just before serving. Serve Hot.

Arctic Char With Blood Orange Salad

Servings: 2
Cooking Time: 10 Minutes

Ingredients:

- 1 filet of arctic char
- 1 lemon, zested
- Salt to taste
- ½ bunch of parsley, picked
- Supremes of 3 blood oranges
- 2 tbsp of olive oil
- 1 radish, sliced
- Salt to taste
- ½ bunch parsley, chopped
- 2 serrano peppers, chopped
- ½ cup of olive oil
- 3 tsp white balsamic vinegar
- 2 cloves garlic, roasted
- 1 lemon, juiced and zested

Directions:

1. Preheat the grill to 400°F using direct heat with a cast iron grate installed.
2. Add the lemon zest to both sides of the arctic char and set aside.
3. Lightly oil the cast iron grate with a basting brush. Remove any excess moisture on the arctic char's skin with a paper towel and add the salt. Cook the fish skin side down for 5 minutes. Flip and cook for another 3-5 minutes. While the fish is cooking prepare your plate by spreading the lemon and herb sauce liberally on the plate. Remove the char from the kamado grill and place the fish flesh side down on the sauce.
4. Serve immediately with the blood orange salad.
5. Mix together all the ingredients for the blood orange salad and set aside.
6. Mix together all the ingredients for the lemon and herb sauce and set aside.

Grilled Lobster

Servings: 4
Cooking Time: 20 Minutes

Ingredients:

- 1/2 bunch of fresh flat-leaf parsley, chopped
- 4 sprigs of fresh thyme, leaves only
- 5 garlic cloves, coarsely chopped
- 1/4 cup unsalted butter, melted
- kosher salt and freshly ground black pepper
- 2 cups panko breadcrumbs
- 2 whole lobsters, about 2lb (1kg) in total, split lengthwise and cleaned at the fish counter
- 2 tbsp olive oil
- lemon wedges, to serve

Directions:

1. Preheat the grill to 400°F (204°C) using direct heat with a cast iron grate installed. In a food processor, combine parsley, thyme, garlic, and butter, and pulse until a cohesive mixture forms. Season with salt and pepper to taste, then add the breadcrumbs and pulse a couple times just to combine.
2. Drizzle lobster with a little oil, then pack the body cavity with the breadcrumb mixture. Place lobsters on the grate shell side down, close the lid, and grill until breadcrumbs are golden brown, about 12 to 18 minutes, keeping the lobster shells between the fire and the tender meat.
3. Remove lobster from the grill, and serve immediately with lemon wedges to squeeze over top.

Clam Bake

Servings: 6
Cooking Time: 30 Minutes

Ingredients:
- 2 lbs mussels, scrubbed and debearded
- 1 1/2 lbs kielbasa sausage, sliced into 1 inch chunks
- 1 1/2 lbs small potatoes (we like red potatoes)
- 2 large onions, roughly chopped
- 2 dozen littleneck clams, scrubbed
- 2 dozen steamer clams, scrubbed
- 2 cups dry white wine
- 2 Tablespoons olive oil
- 1 Tablespoon salt
- 1/2 Tablespoon black pepper

Directions:
1. Preheat the grill to 350°F using direct heat with a cast iron grate installed with the dutch oven on the grid.
2. Add olive oil and onion to the pot and cook until soft, about 5 minutes.
3. Add ingredients in layers in the following order: Kielbasa, Potatoes, Clams, Mussels.
4. Pour in the white wine and cover.
5. Lower the dome for 15-20 minutes or until the potatoes are cooked through and the shellfish have opened up.
6. Ladle out the sausage, potatoes, and seafood and strain the broth, taking care not to get any sand from the clams.
7. Serve on sheets of parchment paper with broth in small bowls for dipping and sipping.
8. If you have never tried parsnips before, they look like a white carrot and taste like a cross between a carrot and horseradish. When they are braised they become sweet, a perfect alternative to plain carrots.

Creole Bbq Shrimp

Servings: 4
Cooking Time: 12 Minutes

Ingredients:
- 1/2 cup Worcestershire sauce
- 2 tbsp fresh lemon juice
- 2 tsp ground black pepper
- 1 tsp minced garlic
- 12 jumbo shrimp, about 1 1/2 lb (680g) in total, heads on and unpeeled
- 1 1/4 cup cold unsalted butter, cut into cubes
- kosher salt
- crusty French bread, to serve
- for the seasoning
- 1 tbsp onion powder
- 1 tbsp garlic powder
- 1 tbsp dried oregano
- 1 tbsp dried basil
- 1 1/2 tsp dried thyme
- 1 1/2 tsp ground black pepper
- 1 1/2 tsp ground white pepper
- 1 1/2 tsp ground cayenne pepper
- 2 1/2 tbsp paprika
- 1 1/2 tbsp kosher salt
- to smoke
- apple, pecan, or hickory wood chunks
- 5 sprigs of fresh rosemary

Directions:

1. Preheat the grill to 400°F (204°C). Once hot, add the wood chunks and rosemary sprigs to the coals. Install the heat deflector and place a cast iron skillet on top.
2. In a medium bowl, combine all the seasoning ingredients. (This makes 10 tbsp Creole seasoning blend. Any extra seasoning can be stored in an airtight container for up to 3 months.)
3. In the hot skillet, combine Worcestershire sauce, lemon juice, pepper, garlic, and 2 tbsp Creole seasoning. Close the grill lid and cook until the liquid begins to simmer, about 2 minutes, then add shrimp. Close the grill lid and cook shrimp until opaque, about 5 to 10 minutes.
4. Remove the skillet from the grill and scatter the butter over top. Gently stir until butter has melted, and season with salt to taste. Serve immediately with crusty French bread.

Smoked Planked Trout

Servings: 4
Cooking Time: 25 Minutes

Ingredients:
- 4 whole trout (12 to 16 ounces each)
- Sea salt and freshly ground black pepper
- 16 whole fresh basil leaves
- 1 lemon, thinly sliced and seeded, plus 4 half lemons for smoking and serving
- 2 tablespoons cold unsalted butter, thinly sliced
- 8 thin slices pancetta or prosciutto

Directions:

1. Preheat the grill to 450°F using direct heat with a cast iron grate installed. Grill the planks until lightly singed on both sides, 2 minutes per side. Let cool.

2. Rinse the trout, inside and out, under cold running water, then blot dry, inside and out, with paper towels. Generously season the trout inside and out with salt and pepper. Place 3 to 4 basil leaves, lemon slices, and butter slices in the cavity of each trout.

3. Tie two pieces of pancetta to each trout, one on top, one on the bottom, using 3 pieces of butchers' string to secure them. Arrange the trout on the grilling planks and place a half lemon on each plank.

4. Meanwhile, adjust the vents on your grill to reduce the temperature to 350°F. (Less air means lower temperatures.) Arrange the planks on the kamado grill grid.

5. Smoke-roast the trout until the pancetta is sizzling and crisp and the trout is cooked through (140°F in the center), 15 to 20 minutes at 350°F.

6. Serve the trout on the planks with the smoked lemons for squeezing.

Grilled Shrimp Cocktail With Fire-roasted Cocktail Sauce

Servings: 4
Cooking Time: 35 Minutes

Ingredients:
- 1 tablespoon olive oil
- 1/2 teaspoon Garlic Salt
- 16 jumbo shrimp (about 1 pound), peeled and deveined 1 cup Fire-Roasted Cocktail Sauce
- 1 tablespoon chopped flat-leaf (Italian) parsley
- 1 lemon, cut into 4 wedges or 8 slices
- 1 cup canned no-salt-added fire-roasted diced tomatoes
- 1 tablespoon horseradish
- 1 tablespoon lime juice
- 1/4 teaspoon Chipotle Puree (optional)

Directions:
1. Preheat the grill to 350°F using direct heat with a cast iron grate installed.
2. Combine the oil and garlic salt in a medium bowl. Add the shrimp and toss well.
3. Skewer the shrimp, place the shrimp on the cooking grid and cook for about 3 minutes on each side, or until pink and firm. Remove from the heat.
4. Spoon 1/4 cup of cocktail sauce into each of 4 decorative glasses. Top with 4 shrimp per glass. Sprinkle with the parsley and garnish with the lemon wedges or slices.
5. Combine all the ingredients in a blender or food processor and puree until smooth. Transfer the sauce to a jar and chill for at least 30 minutes before using to let the flavors meld. The sauce will keep in the refrigerator for about 1 month.

Grilled Oysters

Servings: 2
Cooking Time: 5 Minutes

Ingredients:

- A dozen fresh oysters (the fresher, closer-to-home you can get the better!)
- 6 Tbsp – a little more than half a package – slow-cultured, Roasted Garlic Basil & Parsley Banner Butter
- 1 lemon, cut into slices or wedges
- 3 Tbsp fresh chives, roughly chopped

Directions:

1. Preheat the grill to 425°F using direct heat with a cast iron grate installed.
2. Take your Roasted Garlic Basil & Parsley Banner Butter out of the fridge and set aside in a small bowl.
3. Carefully shuck the oysters with a small knife (an oyster knife with a rounded tip and a work glove on the hand grasping the oyster is a good choice for novice shuckers). Remove the top, flat shell and discard. Place the rounded (bowl side of the shell) side with the oyster on a Perforated Cooking Grid.
4. Place the Perforated Grid in the kamado grill and then add a half tablespoon of softened Roasted Garlic butter to each oyster.
5. Close the lid and kamado grill for 4 or 5 minutes until the oysters are bubbling (not rubbery). The butter should be completely melted and beginning to caramelize on the shell when done.
6. Remove from the kamado grill and move the oysters to a serving plate with the lemons. Squeeze a few wedges/slices onto the oysters and then scatter the chives across the plate.

Grilled Tuna Sandwiches With Chipotle Mayo

Servings: 4
Cooking Time: 2 Minutes

Ingredients:

- 1 tablespoon sesame seeds
- 1 tablespoon good-quality chili powder
- 1 teaspoon salt
- 4 four-ounce tuna steaks
- 4 hamburger buns
- 1 cup mayonnaise
- 3 tablespoons Tabasco Chipotle Sauce
- 4 leaves lettuce
- 4 slices onion
- 4 slices tomato

Directions:

1. In a small bowl, combine the rub ingredients and mix well. Sprinkle the rub evenly on both sides of the tuna steaks.
2. Preheat the grill to 550°F using direct heat with a cast iron grate installed.
3. Place the tuna on the kamado grill for 1 1/2 to 2 minutes, then flip and cook for the same amount on the other side. Most of the tuna should still be red when cut. Remove it to a plate to rest.
4. Quickly toast the buns on the kamado grill.
5. In a small bowl, mix together the mayonnaise with the Tabasco. Spread a thin layer on the top and bottom buns. Put a lettuce leaf on each bun bottom and top with a tuna steak, a slice of onion, a slice of tomato, and the top of the bun.

Grilled Calamari Salad With Lemon Caper Vinaigrette

Servings: 6

Cooking Time: 4 Minutes

Ingredients:
- 2 lbs calamari, cleaned, whole tubes and tentacles
- 1/4 cup olive oil
- 2 Tablespoons mint, roughly chopped
- 1/2 tsp salt
- 1/4 tsp pepper
- 3 cloves garlic, minced
- The juice and zest of 1 lemon
- 8 ounces grape tomatoes, cut in half
- 4 ounces Calamata olives, halved
- 1/2 cup finely chopped red onion
- 1/2 cup mint leaves
- 1/3 cup olive oil
- 2 Tablespoons fresh squeezed lemon juice
- 2 Tablespoons white wine vinegar
- 2 Tablespoons capers in brine, drained
- 1 Tablespoon brown mustard
- 1 (15 ounce) can chickpeas (drained and rinsed)
- 1 cucumber, seeded and roughly chopped

Directions:

1. In a large bowl, whisk together olive oil, mint, garlic, lemon juice and zest, salt, and pepper. Stir in calamari and set aside for 30 minutes.
2. In a separate large bowl, whisk together mustard, lemon juice, vinegar, and olive oil. Add capers and mint and stir to combine.
3. Stir remaining salad ingredients into the dressing and set aside in the refrigerator.
4. Grilling:
5. Preheat the grill to 400°F using direct heat with a cast iron grate installed.
6. Place the calamari directly on the grid for 2 minutes per side. The calamari will curl, that's okay.
7. Remove the calamari from the grill and set aside until cool enough to handle.
8. Slice the tubes into rings and tentacles in half and add to salad. Serve.

Seafood & Smoked Gouda Pasta

Servings: 12
Cooking Time: 40 Minutes

Ingredients:
- 1 red bell pepper, halved
- 4 asparagus stalks
- 8 tbsp olive oil
- 8 garlic cloves, minced
- 2lb (1kg) raw seafood, such as shrimp, scallops, or white fish, thawed if frozen
- kosher salt and freshly ground black pepper
- 16oz (450g) dried vermicelli
- crushed red pepper flakes, to garnish
- chopped fresh flat-leaf parsley, to garnish
- for the sauce
- 2 cups heavy cream
- 1/2 cup unsalted butter, softened
- 1/2 cup grated smoked gouda
- freshly ground black pepper

Directions:

1. Preheat the grill to 350°F (177°C) using direct heat with a cast iron grate installed and a dutch oven on the grate. Place pepper and asparagus on the grate (not in the dutch oven), close the grill lid, and grill until beginning to soften and char, about 7 to 10 minutes. Remove from the grill, chop, and set aside.

2. To the hot dutch oven, add olive oil and garlic. Cook until fragrant, about 30 seconds. Add seafood, season well with salt and pepper, and close the grill lid. Cook until seafood has begun to look opaque and take on color, about 5 minutes, stirring once. Transfer the cooked seafood to a cutting board and return the dutch oven to the grill. Cut seafood into bite-sized pieces. Set aside.

3. To make the sauce, add cream and butter to the hot dutch oven, and whisk gently until butter has melted. Sprinkle in smoked gouda, and stir to incorporate. Season with freshly ground black pepper to taste. Close the grill lid and reduce the cream sauce until just thickened, about 10 minutes, stirring occasionally.

4. On the stovetop, cook vermicelli according to package directions until cooked but still firm to the bite. Drain briefly in a colander.

5. Add seafood, pasta, and vegetables to the dutch oven. Gently toss to coat with the sauce. Garnish with crushed red pepper flakes and parsley. Serve immediately.

Roasted Halibut With Greek Relish

Servings: 6
Cooking Time: 10 Minutes

Ingredients:

- 2 (14.5 ounce) cans of Red Gold Petite Diced Tomatoes, drained
- 1/4 cup extra virgin olive oil
- 3 cloves garlic, minced
- 1/2 tablespoon kosher salt
- 10 fresh basil leaves, chopped
- 10 ounces Kalamata olives, slices 1/4 inch
- 1 small red onion, diced
- 3 ounces feta cheese, dry
- 2 tablespoons red wine vinegar
- 2 tablespoons canola oil, or salad oil of choice
- 2 pounds fresh halibut filets
- Kosher salt and freshly ground black pepper to taste

Directions:

1. For the relish, blend all ingredients, except the halibut, together and refrigerate for a few hours.
2. Preheat the grill to 400°F using direct heat with a cast iron grate installed.
3. Season halibut filets lightly with salt and black pepper.
4. Place seasoned halibut on kamado grill and roast for 8-10 minutes or until the fish just begins to flake.
5. When fish is almost done, place a small amount of the tomato relish on top of the fish and allow to warm through.
6. Remove fish from heat and place it on a small pile of the tomato relish allowing the heat of the fish to warm the tomato relish through. Serve warm.

Festive Kabobs

Servings: 4
Cooking Time: 2 Minutes

Ingredients:

- 1/2 large yellow pepper, washed, cored, seeded and cut in 1-inch squares
- 1/2 large red pepper, washed, cored, seeded and cut in 1-inch squares
- 1 cup mushrooms
- 1/2 cup yellow squash
- 1/2 small red onion, peeled, quartered and separated in layers
- 20 sea scallops (or other)
- Olive oil
- Salt and pepper

Directions:

1. Preheat the grill to 350°F using direct heat with a cast iron grate installed.
2. Prepare kabobs by altering vegetables and scallops on Flexible Skewers.
3. Drizzle kabobs lightly with olive oil and season with salt and pepper.
4. Place kabobs on cooking grid and grill for about 10 minutes, or until scallops are cooked through. Do not overcook or scallops may become tough.
5. Transfer to clean platter; let rest at least 2 min. Serve over rice.

Oysters On The Half Shell

Servings: 4
Cooking Time: 9 Minutes

Ingredients:

- 16 whole oysters
- 1/2 cup butter, softened
- 2 Tablespoons fresh parsley
- 2 cloves garlic, minced
- The zest of 1 lemon

Directions:

1. In a small bowl, combine butter, parsley, garlic, and lemon zest. Set aside
2. Grilling:
3. Preheat the grill to 425°F using direct heat with a cast iron grate installed.
4. Place the cleaned oysters, cup side down, directly on the grids and close the dome for 7-9 minutes or until the oysters open up.
5. Remove the top shells and spoon in equal portions of the compound butter. Close the dome for 1 minute more until the butter melts and serve.

Tuna Artichoke Melt

Servings: 4
Cooking Time: 5 Minutes

Ingredients:

- 8 slices Nature's Own 100% Whole Wheat Bread
- 2 cans (6 ounces each) tuna, drained
- 1/2 cup reduced-fat mayonnaise
- 1/3 cup sliced Kalamata olives
- 1 jar (12 ounces) quartered marinated artichoke hearts
- 8 ounces Manchego cheese, shredded
- 3 plum tomatoes, sliced
- Olive oil

Directions:

1. Preheat the grill to 400°F using direct heat with a cast iron grate installed.
2. Strain artichokes, reserving 1 tablespoon marinade. Cut each artichoke quarter crosswise in half. Combine artichokes, tuna, mayonnaise, olives and reserved marinade in medium bowl.
3. Top each of 4 bread slices with 1/4 cup cheese. Spread 1/4 of tuna mixture evenly over cheese. Top with tomato slices, another 1/4 cup cheese and bread slice; press sandwich together slightly. Brush outside of sandwiches lightly with oil.
4. Cook sandwiches on the griddle 3 to 4 minutes or until browned and cheese melts.

Grilled Lobster Tails With Smoked Caper Cream

Servings: 4

Cooking Time: 5 Minutes

Ingredients:
- 4 Atlantic lobster tails
- 1 cup wagyu beef tallow
- 3½ oz (100 g) sage
- 3½ oz (100 g) lemon thyme
- 1 cup (240 ml) heavy cream (or thickened cream)
- 1 pinch sea salt and freshly ground black pepper
- 1 tbsp (15 ml) capers
- ¾ cup (180 ml) white wine vinegar in a spray bottle
- 2 oz (57 g) finger limes (optional)
- 1 lemon, cut into wedges
- 1 bunch parsley

Directions:
1. Using kitchen shears cut the lobster tail and remove the digestive tract that runs through the meat.
2. Preheat the grill to 500°F using direct heat with a cast iron grate installed.
3. As the kamado grill heats, warm the beef tallow in a Sauce Pan to 175°F; add the sage and lemon thyme to infuse. When the kamado grill reaches cooking temperature, add a cast iron skillet to the grid until hot. Pour in the cream and a pinch of salt and pepper. When the cream on the side of the pan turns a light brown color, slowly use the spoon to stir the cream. When the cream is thick and a brown color, remove the pan from the kamado grill, mix in the capers and set aside.
4. Place the lobster tails side up on the cooking grid. Brush the infused beef tallow over the meat. Spritz the meat with white wine vinegar, then close the dome and cook for 3 to 4 minutes.
5. Move the cooked marron or lobster from the kamado grill; top with caper cream, finger limes, a squeeze of lemon and ice plant or parsley. Add salt and pepper to taste.

Paella On The Egg

Servings: 6
Cooking Time: 10 Minutes

Ingredients:

- ½ cup canola or vegetable oil
- Kosher salt and freshly ground black pepper
- 10 cups chicken stock
- 1 large pinch saffron
- 2 pounds clams, scrubbed
- 2 pounds mussels, de-bearded and scrubbed
- 18 colossal shrimp, peeled
- Two 2-pound lobsters, par-cooked in salted boiling water for about 12 minutes, drained well and halved lengthwise
- 15 sea scallops, patted dry
- 4 lemons, halved
- 1 large Spanish onion, finely chopped
- 6 cloves garlic, finely chopped
- 4 cups short grain paella rice
- 1-pound Spanish chorizo (Paul uses ½ sweet and ½ spicy), sliced into ½ in thick slices
- 1 cup frozen peas, thawed
- 1 jar piquillo peppers, thinly sliced (6 or 8 peppers)
- 1 cup chopped fresh flat-leaf parsley (optional)

Directions:

1. Preheat the grill to 400°F using direct heat with a cast iron grate installed. Add the dutch oven to the grid to preheat.
2. Combine chicken stock and saffron in the dutch oven and bring to a simmer. Add the clams, cover and cook until the clams open, about 8 to 10 minutes. Remove the clams to a bowl. Add the mussels to the broth, cover and cook until the mussels open, about 5 minutes. Transfer to a bowl. Make sure to discard any shellfish that didn't open up. Remove the dutch oven from the grill.
3. Brush the shrimp, scallops, the cut sides of the lobsters and cut sides of the lemons with some of the oil and sprinkle with salt and pepper on all sides. Grill the shrimp for about 1 minute per side. Grill the lobster cut-side down until charred and just cooked through, about 5 minutes. Remove the claws and the tails but leave the shells on; discard the bodies. Grill the scallops until slightly charred and almost cooked through, about 1 minute per side. Grill the lemon cut-side down until charred, about 45 seconds. Remove all ingredients to sheet pans or disposable drip pans and set aside.
4. Heat 3 tablespoons canola oil in a wok or paella pan over direct heat. Add the onions and cook until soft. Add the garlic and cook for 1 minute. Add the chorizo and cook, stirring occasionally, until brown and crisp, about 5 minutes.
5. Add the rice and cook, stirring constantly, for a few minutes, letting the rice absorb the oils from the chorizo. Begin adding the stock 1 cup at a time and cook, stirring constantly, until the rice is al dente, about 20-25 minutes.
6. Arrange the clam, mussels, shrimp, scallop, peas, lobster and piquillo peppers on the rice. Squeeze the juice from 4 of the lemon halves over the top, and nestle the 4 other halves in the rice. Scatter the parsley over the top. Stir gently to bring some of the rice up from the bottom. Serve while warm.

Lemon Bed Cod

Servings: 6

Cooking Time: 15 Minutes

Ingredients:

- 6 cod filets
- 3 lemons, sliced 1/4 inch thick
- 1 onion, thinly sliced
- Salt & Pepper to taste

Directions:

1. Place lemon slices directly on the grid so they are shingled one on top of another.
2. Place onion slices on top of the lemon.
3. Grilling:
4. Preheat the grill to 400°F using direct heat with a cast iron grate installed.
5. Season both sides of the cod filets with salt and pepper and place them on top of the onion and lemon beds.
6. Close the dome for 12-15 minutes to allow the lemons to steam the fish.
7. Remove the fish on their lemon beds when the fish is opaque. Serve.

Southwest Baked Oysters

Servings:2

Cooking Time: 15 Minutes

Ingredients:

- Clean oyster shells
- Olive oil
- Oysters
- Finely chopped jalapeno chiles
- Shredded cheddar cheese or grated parmesan cheese
- Bacon bits or soy bacon bits
- Italian-style seasoned bread crumbs

Directions:

1. Preheat the grill to 375°F using direct heat with a cast iron grate installed.
2. Arrange they oyster shells in a Perforated Cooking Grid. Spray with olive oil. Place 1 large or 2 small oysters in each shell. Top each with 2 or 3 tiny pieces of jalapeno. Sprinkle with cheese and bacon bits. Top with bread crumbs.
3. Place pan on the cooking grid and bake at 375° for 10 to 15 minutes or until bubbly; do not overcook.

Bourbon-glazed Cold Smoked Salmon

Servings: 8
Cooking Time: 210 Minutes

Ingredients:
- 2-pound salmon filet, skin on
- 1 tablespoon Makers Mark Bourbon
- 1 orange, zested and sliced into rings
- 1 cup kosher salt
- 2 cups dark brown sugar
- 1 cup Makers Mark Bourbon
- 1/3 cup brown sugar
- ½ cup fig jam
- 1 Tbsp orange juice
- 2 tsp Worcestershire sauce
- ¼ tsp dried mustard
- Pinch of garlic

Directions:

1. Lay the salmon skin-side down on a cutting board. Remove any bones from the flesh and wipe clean of scales. Rinse the salmon with the whiskey and allow to air dry for 10 minutes.
2. In a bowl, combine orange zest, salt and sugar. Line a baking dish with plastic wrap, extending the wrap to allow for wrapping the salmon later. Sprinkle half of the salt mixture on the plastic wrap. Add the salmon and cover with the remaining salt mixture.
3. Lay the orange slices on top of the mixture. Wrap the salmon tightly in the plastic wrap and place in the back of your refrigerator for 48 hours.
4. Once cured, rinse the salmon in cold water. Place the salmon back into the refrigerator, uncovered, for 4 hours.
5. For the glaze, bring bourbon to a boil over medium heat in a saucepan. Add the sugar and whisk, add the remaining ingredients, whisking to blend after each addition. Reduce heat to simmer until sauce is thickened and reduced by half.
6. Preheat the grill to 50°F using direct heat with a cast iron grate installed. Add the salmon to the grid and smoke for 1 hour. Baste the salmon with the bourbon glaze and smoke for an additional 2½ hours.
7. Slice and serve with crackers.

Mediterranean Surf And Turf Kabobs

Servings: 6
Cooking Time: 20 Minutes

Ingredients:
- 1 lb. boneless leg of lamb (cut into 1 x 1 pieces)
- 1 lb. jumbo shrimp (peeled and deveined)
- 1 red onion (cut into 1 x 1 chunks)
- 1 container baby portobello mushrooms
- 1 container grape tomatoes
- 1 can artichoke hearts
- 1 cup olive oil
- ¼ cup red wine vinegar
- ¼ cup capers (chopped)
- 2 tbsp. fresh oregano (chopped)
- 2 tbsp. fresh rosemary (chopped)
- 2 tbsp. thyme (chopped)
- 1-2 cloves garlic (chopped)
- 1-2 tsp. kosher salt
- ½ tsp. ground black pepper
- ½ tsp. cumin
- ½ tsp. ground coriander

Directions:
1. Preheat the grill to 425°F using direct heat with a cast iron grate installed.
2. You will make 2 different skewers – one will hold the lamb, mushrooms, shrimp and onions. The other will have tomatoes and artichokes. Place the skewers in a pan or dish and pour marinade over them. Toss skewers in marinade and allow marinating for up to 1 hour.
3. Grill the lamb/shrimp skewer for 7-10 minutes or until cooked thoroughly (suggested internal temperature is 135°F). Grill the tomato/artichoke skewer for 3-5 minutes. Take the grilled items off the skewer and serve with either rice or couscous with Tzatziki sauce for a delicious meal!
4. Combine all of the ingredients for the marinade. Set aside.

Seared Ahi Tuna

Servings: 2
Cooking Time: 6 Minutes

Ingredients:

- 2 ahi tuna steaks
- ¼ cup soy sauce
- 1 teaspoon corn starch
- ¼ cup pineapple juice
- ¼ cup honey
- 1 teaspoon sriracha
- 2 tablespoons sesame seeds, toasted

Directions:

1. Preheat the grill to 500°F using direct heat with a cast iron grate installed. Mix soy sauce and cornstarch until smooth. Add pineapple juice, honey and sriracha. Place pot on stove over medium heat and bring to a boil. Reduce heat and simmer 3-4 minutes until the thickened. Remove from heat.
2. Heat cast iron skillet and add oil. Sear tuna steaks 1-2 minutes, brushing each side with sauce mixture after searing. Garnish with sesame seeds.

Cedar Planked Salmon With Honey Glaze

Servings: 4
Cooking Time: 18 Minutes

Ingredients:

- 2 Cedar Grilling Planks
- ½ cup (120 ml) Dijon mustard
- ¼ cup (60 ml) honey
- 1 tbsp (15 ml) balsamic vinegar
- 2 tsp (10 ml) grated orange zest
- 1 tsp (5 ml) minced fresh thyme plus extra for garnish
- 2 tbsp (30 ml) extra-virgin olive oil
- 4 (7 ounce/200 g) salmon fillets, skin on
- Kosher salt and freshly ground black pepper

Directions:

1. Place the planks in a pan, cover with water and let soak for at least one hour and up to eight hours.
2. Preheat the grill to 400°F using direct heat with a cast iron grate installed.
3. Whisk together the mustard, honey, balsamic vinegar, orange zest, and 1 teaspoon thyme.
4. Place the planks on the grid, close the lid of the kamado grill and preheat for 3 minutes. Open the lid and turn the planks over, brush with the olive oil, and place 2 salmon fillets on each plank. Season with salt and pepper and brush generously with the honey glaze. Cook for 12 to 15 minutes for medium.
5. Remove from the heat and garnish with thyme. Pair with a glass of Spellbound Chardonnay.

Cold-smoked Rock Shrimp

Servings: 6
Cooking Time: 20 Minutes

Ingredients:
- 2 lb. rock shrimp
- 2 qt. ice
- ½ cup rock salt
- 3 sprigs of parsley
- 3 sprigs of tarragon
- 2 radishes, sliced
- Juice/zest of 6 blood oranges
- 1 cup cider vinegar
- ½ cup sugar
- 1 garlic clove, minced
- ½ tsp Aleppo pepper, or chili of your choice

Directions:
1. Preheat the grill to 250°F using direct heat with a cast iron grate installed.
2. Prep the shrimp by placing them on top of a perforated pan or in aluminum foil with a few holes poked through. Place this pan over an ice/rock salt mixture inside a non-perforated pan.
3. Place ½ of the herbs on the charcoal and ½ on the cooking grid, then add the pan with the shrimp to the kamado grill and cold-smoke for 20 minutes; the shrimp will not be fully cooked.
4. To serve, place some gastrique in the bottom of a bowl, top with shrimp, add some raw radishes and herbs to the top and enjoy!
5. Mix all the gastrique ingredients together and cook until slightly syrupy. Cool, pour over the shrimp, and let marinate for one hour before serving.

Grilled Oysters With Garlic Butter

Servings: 4
Cooking Time: 5 Minutes

Ingredients:
- A dozen fresh oysters (the fresher, closer-to-home you can get the better!)
- 6 Tbsp – a little more than half a package – slow-cultured, Roasted Garlic Basil & Parsley Banner Butter
- 1 lemon, cut into slices or wedges
- 3 Tbsp fresh chives, roughly chopped

Directions:
1. Preheat the grill to 425°F using direct heat with a cast iron grate installed.
2. Take your Roasted Garlic Basil & Parsley Banner Butter out of the fridge and set aside in a small bowl.
3. Carefully shuck the oysters with a small knife (an oyster knife with a rounded tip and a work glove on the hand grasping the oyster is a good choice for novice shuckers). Remove the top, flat shell and discard. Place the rounded (bowl side of the shell) side with the oyster on a Perforated Cooking Grid.
4. Place the Perforated Grid in the kamado grill and then add a half tablespoon of softened Roasted Garlic butter to each oyster.
5. Close the lid and kamado grill for 4 or 5 minutes until the oysters are bubbling (not rubbery). The butter should be completely melted and beginning to caramelize on the shell when done.
6. Remove from the kamado grill and move the oysters to a serving plate with the lemons. Squeeze a few wedges/slices onto the oysters and then scatter the chives across the plate.

POULTRY

Smoked Spanish Chicken

Servings: 8
Cooking Time: 180 Minutes

Ingredients:
- 4-5lb all natural whole chicken
- 4 oz fresh chorizo sausage
- 1 can Landshark Lager
- 1 dried ancho chili
- 1 small lime, cut into 8 wedges
- 1 tsp whole black peppercorns
- 1 tsp smoked sweet paprika
- 1/2 tsp cumin
- 1/2 tsp chili powder
- 1 tsp cayenne pepper
- 1 1/2 tsp granulated garlic
- 1 1/2 tsp onion powder
- 2 tbs sea salt
- 1 tbs fresh ground black pepper
- 2 tablespoons of olive oil

Directions:

1. Pop open a can of Landshark and empty about half the liquid (Rusty recommends taking a few sips). Remove the pop-top and fill can with lime slices, onion and dried ancho peppers, seeds and all. Add black peppercorns and shake can.

2. Pat and dry chicken. Stuff most of the chorizo underneath the skin of the chicken. Take the last bit of chorizo and stuff in the neck area; it will self-baste as the chicken roasts.

3. Mix together cayenne pepper, cumin, garlic, powdered onion, paprika, chili powder, salt and pepper. Press and rub onto the skin of the chicken. Place Landshark can inside the chicken carcass and stand it up in foil pan to contain the drippings.

4. Place foil pan on the cooking grid of the kamado grill (you can smoke with apple or cherry wood for extra flavor) and cook for 2-1/2 to 2-3/4 hours at temperature of 315 to 325°F. Use a meat thermometer to thoroughly cook chicken. Remove beer can, let chicken rest for about 15 minutes and cut in half. Serve with fresh vegetables or green salad, and enjoy, compliments of Chef Rusty!

Hatch Chile Salsa And Chicken Casserole

Servings: 6

Cooking Time: 55 Minutes

Ingredients:

- 5 boneless, skinless chicken breasts
- 32 oz. shredded cheddar cheese
- 32 oz. chicken stock
- 5-6 large tortillas
- ¼ cup Cotija cheese
- 15-20 Hatch chiles
- 1 small onion or ½ large onion
- 4 cloves garlic
- 1 bunch cilantro
- 1 tsp cumin
- ½ tsp coriander
- 2 limes, juiced
- 2 tsp honey
- Salt to taste

Directions:

1. Preheat the grill to 400°F using direct heat with a cast iron grate installed.
2. In the dutch oven, cover the chicken with chicken broth and 2 tbsp of the hatch chile salsa. Place on the grill and simmer until the internal temperature reaches 165°F, about 15 minutes. Remove from the grill, strain and chop the chicken.
3. In the same dutch oven, spread a tablespoon of salsa on the bottom. Next place a tortilla and top with chicken and a handful of cheese. Repeat this process until the ingredients are gone. Place on the grill and bake for 20 minutes or until the cheese is melted. During the last 5 minutes top with the Cotija cheese. Remove from the kamado grill and let rest for 10-15 minutes. Enjoy!
4. Preheat the grill to 400°F using direct heat with a cast iron grate installed.
5. Roast the Hatch chiles for 5 minutes per side or until there is a charred outside. Remove the chiles from the grill and place in a gallon-sized resealable bag for 10-15 minutes. The chiles should be soft and pliable at this point. Remove the skins, stems and seeds from the chiles.
6. To give the salsa even more of a roasted flavor you can also roast the onion, garlic and lime, however, this is an optional step. Put all the ingredients for the salsa in a blender or a food processor and blend together to desired consistency. Set aside.

Butter-injected Turkey And Sides

Servings: 16
Cooking Time: 350 Minutes

Ingredients:

- 1 12-14 lb. whole turkey
- 5 oz. Roasted Garlic & Herb Banner Butter, melted
- 1 orange, cut into wedges
- 1 sweet onion, cut into wedges
- 1 lemon, cut into wedges
- 2 whole heads of garlic, top cut off
- 3 sprigs rosemary
- 3 sprigs thyme
- 3 sprigs sage
- Savory Pecan Seasoning
- Extra virgin olive oil or canola oil
- Kosher salt
- 6 whole carrots
- ½ lb. red potatoes cut in half
- 8 oz whole baby Portobello mushrooms
- 2 zucchinis, cut into ½ inch strips
- 8 oz cherry tomatoes
- 8 oz green beans
- 5 oz. Fig & Balsamic Banner Butter, melted
- 2 tbsp extra virgin olive oil
- ½ tbsp kosher salt
- ¼ tbsp cracked black pepper
- 2 tbsp Worcestershire sauce
- 4 sweet potatoes
- 2 tbsp brown sugar
- ½ tbsp kosher salt
- ½ cup butter

Directions:

1. Preheat the grill to 350°F using direct heat with a cast iron grate installed.
2. Pat the turkey dry and coat with oil, season with salt and Savory Pecan Seasoning. Pull melted butter into the injector and evenly inject the turkey with the butter (to prevent splash back from the injector, cover the turkey with plastic wrap and inject the turkey through the plastic wrap.)
3. Place half of the onion, one whole head of garlic, half the orange, half the lemon, and two sprigs of each herb inside the cavity of the turkey. Fold the wings back behind the turkey so that they cook evenly. Add the remaining garlic, onion, orange, lemon and herbs around the turkey in the drip pan.
4. Place on the grill and cook 3-4 hours or until the internal temperature is 165°F (white meat) and 185°F (dark meat). During the cook, cover the turkey with aluminum foil once the skin has the desired color and texture.
5. Remove from the grill, let rest for 15 minutes. Carve and enjoy!
6. Preheat the grill to 350°F using direct heat with a cast iron grate installed.
7. Coat the dutch oven lid with extra virgin olive oil. Place all vegetables into the dutch oven lid. In a bowl, mix melted butter, Worcestershire sauce, pepper and salt. Pour evenly over the top of the vegetables.
8. Roast for 45 minutes, remove from the grill and serve.
9. Preheat the grill to 350°F using direct heat with a cast iron grate installed.
10. Poke holes in the sweet potato, all over. Bake until soft and skin has blistered – about 50 minutes to an hour.
11. Remove from the grill and let rest for 10 minutes. Peel the skin off and discard. Place in a bowl and mash the sweet potatoes. Add salt, and butter and mix thoroughly. Enjoy!

Beer Can Chicken

Servings: 6
Cooking Time: 60 Minutes

Ingredients:
- 1 (4-5 lb) chicken
- 1/4 cup Country Style Rub
- 1 (12-ounce) beer in a can
- 1 sprig rosemary
- 2 cloves garlic, smashed

Directions:
1. Open the beer, drink half.
2. Add rosemary and garlic cloves to the remaining beer.
3. Sprinkle Country Style Rub on every surface, inside and out, of the chicken.
4. Situate the chicken on top of the beer can until the can is firmly inside of the cavity.
5. Grilling:
6. Preheat the grill to 375°F using direct heat with a cast iron grate installed.
7. Place the chicken with the beer can standing up on the grid.
8. Close the dome and allow the chicken to cook for 45 minutes to 1 hour or until the internal temperature of the thigh reaches 170°F.
9. Allow the chicken to rest of the heat for 10 minutes before removing the beer can and carving.
10. To cut the spine out of a chicken is called to "spatchcock". This not only allows you to place a brick on top of the bird, but also speeds up the cooking process. Using kitchen shears, cut up one side of the spine and down the other removing it completely. Then, flip the chicken breast side up and press firmly to flatten.

Garfunkel Chicken

Servings: 6
Cooking Time: 50 Minutes

Ingredients:
- 1 whole young chicken, 3 to 4 pounds
- 1/2 cup olive oil
- 1 tbsp parsley
- 1 tbsp rubbed sage
- 1 tbsp rosemary
- 1 tsp ground thyme
- 1/2 tsp salt
- 1/2 tsp black pepper

Directions:
1. Remove the backbone from the chicken with either poultry shears or a sharp knife. Turn the chicken over and press down to flatten and break the cartilage in the breast. Rub the entire bird with the olive oil. Mix the herbs and spices together and sprinkle these over the entire bird.
2. Preheat the grill to 350°F using direct heat with a cast iron grate installed. Cook the chicken skin side down for about 15 to 20 minutes until the skin is browned and crispy.
3. Flip the chicken over to bone side down and cook for another 25 to 30 minutes until the internal temperature in the breast is 160°F.

Rotisserie Style Chicken

Servings: 4
Cooking Time: 60 Minutes

Ingredients:

- 1 (4-5 lb) whole chicken
- 1/2 recipe Turkey Brine
- 1 cup White Barbecue Sauce

Directions:

1. Place chicken in Turkey Brine for 2 hours or overnight.
2. Rinse the chicken and pat dry.
3. Grilling:
4. Preheat the grill to 375°F using direct heat with a cast iron grate installed.
5. Place the chicken on the grids, breast side up, and close the dome for 20 minutes.
6. Flip the chicken over and cook for an additional 20 minutes.
7. Baste the chicken with White Barbecue Sauce, flip the chicken, and replace the dome for 5 minutes.
8. Repeat until the internal temperature of the thigh reaches 170°F.
9. Allow the chicken to rest off the heat for 10 minutes before carving.

Bacon Wrapped Jalapeño Stuffed Chicken Thighs

Servings: 6
Cooking Time: 30 Minutes

Ingredients:

- 8 boneless, skinless chicken thighs
- 4 jalapeño peppers
- 8 oz cream cheese
- 16 strips of bacon
- 1 stick of butter
- All-Purpose Rub
- Sweet and Smoky seasoning
- 1 cup salt
- 1/2 cup granulated garlic
- 1/4 cup black pepper

Directions:

1. Preheat the grill to 375°F using direct heat with a cast iron grate installed. If desired, add some pecan chips for some extra smokiness.
2. Remove the thighs from the packaging and place on a cutting board designated for poultry. Trim any excess fat on the thighs and season each side with a hefty dose of Sweet and Smoky seasoning.
3. Cut the jalapeño peppers in half lengthwise and remove the seeds and veins. Fill each half with cream cheese and sprinkle a touch of all-purpose rub on top.
4. Place the stuffed jalapeño peppers cheese side down in the center of each chicken thigh and form the meat around the pepper. Next, wrap each thigh with 2 strips of bacon.
5. Place the wrapped chicken thigh in a Drip Pan, and top each piece of chicken with a pat of butter. Cook for 30 minutes, until chicken reaches an internal temperature of 165°F.
6. Remove from the kamado grill and let the chicken rest for 8-10 minutes, sprinkle more Sweet and Smoky seasoning on the chicken and spoon some of the butter sauce over the chicken.
7. Serve immediately.
8. Mix all the ingredients together and set aside.

Chicken Keema Burgers

Servings: 4
Cooking Time: 12 Minutes

Ingredients:
- 2 lbs ground chicken
- 1/2 cup fresh breadcrumbs
- 1 Tablespoon olive oil
- 2 cloves garlic, finely chopped
- 1 small onion, finely chopped
- 1 egg
- 4 pieces Naan
- 2 Tablespoons Indian Spice Rub
- 1/2 cup Greek style yogurt
- 1/2 cup finely chopped, seeded, cucumber
- 2 Tablespoons chopped fresh cilantro
- 1 tsp finely chopped green onion
- 1/4 tsp ground cumin

Directions:

1. In a small bowl, combine ingredients for the raita and set aside. The raita can be made a day in advance, covered, and refrigerated.
2. In a small skillet, heat olive oil over medium and add onion and garlic. Cook until soft and translucent. Set aside to cool.
3. In a medium bowl, combine ground chicken, bread crumbs, onion mixture, egg, and Indian Spice Rub until combined. Form 4 patties and return to the fridge to chill for 10 minutes.
4. Grilling:
5. Preheat the grill to 500°F using direct heat with a cast iron grate installed.
6. Place burgers on the grid and close the dome for 3 minutes.
7. Flip burgers and close the dome for 3 more minutes.
8. Close all of the vents and allow the burgers to sit for 5-6 minutes or until the internal temperature reaches 170°F.
9. Serve burgers on naan, topped with raita.

Grilled Hot Candy Chicken Wings

Servings:4

Cooking Time: 30 Minutes

Ingredients:
- 5 pounds Springer Mountain Farms Chicken Wings split chicken wings, rinsed and dried
- ¼ cup Sweet & Smoky Seasoning
- 2 tbsp seasoned salt
- 2 tbsp cooking oil
- 2 cups Kansas City Style BBQ Sauce
- ½ cup hot sauce
- 1 cup honey
- ½ cup ground cinnamon

Directions:

1. Preheat the grill to 350°F using direct heat with a cast iron grate installed with hickory wood chips. Grill for about 30 minutes or until the internal temperature reached 165°F or higher. Turn the wings occasionally for even cooking.

2. For the dry rub, mix the barbecue rub and seasoned salt into a bowl and blend well. Place the chicken wings in a large resealable plastic bag. Pour in the dry rub and oil, shake to coat the wings well. Marinate overnight in the refrigerator.

3. For the Hot Candy Sauce, mix the ingredients well. Coat the cooked wings with the sauce and serve.

Smokey Thai Pulled Chicken Sandwiches

Servings: 6
Cooking Time: 92 Minutes

Ingredients:

- 3 lbs boneless skinless chicken thighs
- 1 package of Cobblestone Bread Co.™ Sesame Twist Hamburger Rolls
- 3 tbs chopped cilantro
- quick pickled carrots
- * optional Sriracha sauce
- 3 cups water
- 2 tbs pure cane sugar
- juice of one lime
- 2 tsp Thai fish sauce
- 2 tsp soy sauce
- 1 tbs sea salt
- 1-2 hot peppers (Thai bird or Serrano)
- 2 cloves of garlic
- 1 tbs pure cane sugar
- 2 tsp sea salt
- 1 tsp onion powder
- ½ tsp ground ginger
- ½ tsp garlic powder
- ¼ tsp ground white pepper
- ¼ cup water
- ¼ cup honey
- 1 tbs fresh lime juice
- 2 tbs soy sauce
- 1 tsp Thai fish sauce (add while mixing, do not heat)
- ⅔ pound carrots
- 2½ cups water
- ⅔ cup rice wine vinegar
- 1 tbs pure cane sugar
- 2 tsp sea salt
- 2 tsp fresh grated ginger

Directions:

1. Whisk together ingredients for the brine. Add the chicken thighs, making sure they are fully covered. Place in refrigerator for 2-3 hours.
2. About a half hour before you are ready to grill. Preheat the grill to 280°F using direct heat with a cast iron grate installed.
3. Whisk together the dry rub ingredients. Remove the chicken thighs from brine, and pat dry. Discard brine. Generously coat the chicken with dry rub.
4. Place chicken thighs on the kamado grill. Cook for 1½ hours, flipping once after about 50 minutes. Check temperature occasionally to make sure you are not gout over a maximum of 325°F, damper more narrowly to reduce temperature closer to 280°F.
5. Prepare the Quick Pickled Carrots while the chicken is grilling.
6. When chicken thighs are removed from the kamado grill, set aside to rest and cool a little, then pull the chicken (discard any fatty bits). Mix in chopped fresh cilantro.
7. Mix sauce ingredients, except fish sauce, in a small saucepan over medium-high heat. Once it comes to a boil, reduce to a simmer. Allow to gently bubble for 2 minutes, then shut off and pour over the pulled chicken. Mix. Add fish sauce and mix again.

8. Place some of the pickled matchstick carrots on the bottom half of each Cobblestone Bread Co.™ Sesame Twist Hamburger Roll. Top with a generous helping of the Thai pulled chicken (squirt on a bit of sriracha sauce if you like) and cover with top of the roll.
9. Peel and trim carrots, then matchstick slice.
10. Whisk together pickling brine ingredients in a deep microwave-safe bowl. Microwave for 2 minutes, then whisk again to ensure salt & sugar are dissolved. Add the carrots. Make sure they are fully covered in the brine.
11. Microwave until the brine come to a quick boil (about 5-6 minutes). Microwave for another minute (you may need to stop it a couple times to avoid boil over). Remove from the microwave and set aside to cool.
12. When the brine has cooled to room temperature, drain. Refrigerate the carrots until ready to go on sandwiches.

Chicken & Veggie Stir-fry

Servings: 6
Cooking Time: 10 Minutes

Ingredients:
- 2 tablespoons toasted sesame oil
- 1½ teaspoons plus 1½ teaspoons minced garlic
- 1½ teaspoons plus 1½ teaspoons minced fresh ginger
- 2 pounds boneless, skinless chicken breasts, cubed
- ½ cup rice wine
- ½ cup light soy sauce
- ½ cup chicken stock
- ¼ cup hoisin sauce
- 2 tablespoons rice wine vinegar
- 2 tablespoons granulated sugar
- 2 tablespoons cornstarch
- 1 teaspoon chili garlic sauce (optional)
- ½ cup canola oil
- 4 cups broccoli florets
- 1 cup broccoli stems, trimmed and julienned
- 1 cup julienned carrots
- 1 cup drained water chestnuts, diced
- 1 tablespoon toasted sesame seeds

Directions:
1. Preheat the grill to 500°F using direct heat with a cast iron grate installed.
2. Combine the sesame oil, 1½ teaspoons of the garlic, and 1½ teaspoons of the ginger in a small bowl, add the chicken, and toss to coat. Let the chicken marinate for 30 minutes.
3. To make the sauce, mix the remaining 1½ teaspoons garlic, 1½ teaspoons ginger, rice wine, soy sauce, chicken stock, hoisin sauce, rice wine vinegar, sugar, cornstarch, and chili garlic sauce in a small bowl. Set aside.
4. Place a Carbon Steel Wok on the spander and preheat for 2 minutes.
5. Place the canola oil and chicken in the wok. Close the lid of the kamado grill and cook for 5 to 6 minutes, until seared on all sides. Add the broccoli florets and stems, carrots, and water chestnuts and cook for 2 to 3 minutes, stirring well. Add the sauce and continue to cook until the sauce has thickened. Remove the wok from the kamado grill.
6. Transfer the stir-fry to a bowl and garnish with the sesame seeds.

Chimichurri Smoked Chicken Salad Sandwich

Servings: 2
Cooking Time: 30 Minutes

Ingredients:
- 2 chicken breast
- 2 tbsp olive oil
- ½ tbsp garlic salt
- Apple wood chips, soaked
- 2 Cobblestone Bread Co.™ Toasted Onion Rolls
- 2 smoked chicken breasts, chopped
- 2 tbsp mayo
- 1 tbsp chimichurri
- 1 tbsp grilled corn
- 1 tbsp chopped peppadews
- Salt and lime to taste

Directions:
1. Add the chicken to a ziplock bag and add garlic salt and olive oil. Let it sit for at least two hours.
2. Prepare the grill by placing a small handful of soaked apple wood chips and Natural Lump Charcoal in the bottom of the kamado grill and light it with a Fire Starter. Place the platesetter with the legs facing up and add the metal grate. Close the kamado grill and try to regulate the heat around 340ºF/171ºC. Do this by opening the top vent a half inch and adjusting the bottom vent so that a little over an inch is exposed. Watch your kamado grill for about an hour so that it has time to regulate without getting too hot. Add the chicken and let it smoke for about 30 minutes or until the internal temperature of 160ºF is reached. Remove from heat and let cool.
3. Once the chicken salad has been prepared, simply toast the Cobblestone Bread Co.™ Toasted Onion Rolls on the kamado grill for a few minutes and fill each roll with half of the chicken salad. Serve.
4. Add mayo and the chimichurri to a medium sized bowl and stir to combine. Add chopped chicken, grilled corn, and peppadews. Season with salt and lime to taste and set aside.

Grilled Vidalia Onion Chicken Peach Skewers

Servings: 4
Cooking Time: 10 Minutes

Ingredients:
- 1 large Springer Mountain Farms chicken breast
- 2 Tablespoons fresh lime or lemon juice
- 2 Tablespoons sunflower or canola oil
- Salt and pepper
- ½ Vidalia onion, cut in 1" pieces
- 1 Peach, pitted, cut in 1 "pieces
- Fresh basil
- Bamboo Skewers

Directions:
1. Preheat the grill to 350°F using direct heat with a cast iron grate installed.
2. Soak skewers in water for 30 minutes before using. Slice chicken on bias in thin pieces. Marinate chicken in a bowl with lime or lemon juice, oil, salt and pepper for 10-20 minutes.
3. Weave chicken with peaches and Vidalia onions onto skewers (you can cut chicken and just alternate with peaches and onions).
4. Grill skewers about 4-5 minutes per side. While skewers are cooking melt jelly in microwave. Brush skewers on both sides when you turn them. Garnish with fresh basil cut in ribbons.

Rotisserie Chicken

Servings: 6
Cooking Time: 90 Minutes

Ingredients:
- 1 (4-5 lb) whole chicken, gizzards and giblets removed
- 2 quarts warm water
- 1/4 cup kosher salt
- 1/4 cup brown sugar
- 2 Tablespoons whole peppercorns
- 1 lemon, halved
- 2 lbs small waxy potatoes, cut in half (we like Yukon golds)
- 1 lbs carrots, cut into 2 inch chunks
- 1/4 cup butter, softened
- 1 onion, cut into wedges
- 2 sprigs fresh thyme
- 4 whole cloves garlic

Directions:
1. Combine brine ingredients until the salt and sugar dissolve and add enough ice to bring the brine to room temperature.
2. Submerge the chicken into the brine and allow to chill in the refrigerator for a minimum of 2 hours and up to overnight.
3. Remove the chicken from the brine and pat dry.
4. In the bottom of a cold dutch oven, place the vegetables and top with the chicken, breast side up.
5. Gently lift the skin away from the meat and rub butter beneath the skin.
6. Grilling:
7. Preheat the grill to 425°F using direct heat with a cast iron grate installed.
8. Cover the dutch oven and place on the grill. Lower the dome for 1-1 1/2 hours or until the internal temperature of the meatiest part of the thigh registers 160°F
9. Remove the dutch oven from the grill and allow it to sit for an additional 10 minutes before removing the lid.
10. Remove the chicken, place the vegetables on a platter or in a bowl. Carve the chicken and serve.

Barbecue Chicken With Alabama White Sauce

Servings: 4
Cooking Time: 40 Minutes

Ingredients:

- 4 egg yolks
- ¼ cup apple cider vinegar
- ¼ cup water
- 2 tablespoons poultry seasoning
- 2 tablespoons salt
- 1 cup grapeseed oil
- 6 chicken leg/thigh pieces
- approx. 1 ½ cups Alabama white barbecue sauce
- 2 egg yolks
- ¼ cup lemon juice
- 3 tablespoons apple cider vinegar
- 2 teaspoons salt
- ½ teaspoon garlic powder
- ½ teaspoon cayenne pepper
- 2 teaspoons ground black pepper
- 1 cup grapeseed oil

Directions:

1. In a food processor fitted with a metal blade, blend the egg yolks, vinegar, water, poultry seasoning, and salt until the yolks fluff a little, about 30 seconds. With the processor running, slowly drizzle in the oil, the mixture will blend, emulsify, and resemble a thick mayonnaise. You will hear the sound change to a whop, whop; it should take about 1 minute. Spoon the marinade into a large zip-top bag, add the chicken pieces, and massage until the chicken is completely covered with the marinade. Zip the top closed, pressing out any air as you seal the bag. Set the bag in a bowl in the refrigerator overnight or for up to 24 hours.

2. Pour ¾ cup of the Alabama white barbecue sauce into a bowl to use for basting. Preheat the grill to 400°F using direct heat with a cast iron grate installed. Remove the chicken from the marinade and pat completely dry. Scrape the cooking grid clean and coat with oil. Place the chicken, skin side down, on the grid and cover with an aluminum drip pan or tent with foil. After 10 minutes, flip the chicken pieces. Cover again with the pan or foil. After 10 more minutes, baste the chicken with the sauce, flip so the skin side is down, and baste again. Cover with the pan or foil, cook for another 10 minutes, and then baste, flip, and cover again. Cook, baste, flip, and cover one last time, for a total cooking time of 40 minutes. Discard the basting sauce. Remove the chicken from the grill and rest, tented with foil or a foil pan, for 10 minutes. Serve with remaining sauce on the side.

3. In a food processor fitted with a metal blade, combine the egg yolks, lemon juice, vinegar, salt, garlic powder, cayenne, and black pepper and process until the yolks fluff a little, about 30 seconds. With the processor running, slowly drizzle in the oil; the mixture will blend and emulsify but won't be as thick as the marinade used for the barbecue chicken. You will again hear the sound change to a whop, whop; it should take about a minute.

Caribbean Chicken Thigh Kebabs

Servings: 4
Cooking Time: 12 Minutes

Ingredients:
- 1 lb. boneless chicken thighs, cut into 1-inch pieces
- ⅓ cup orange juice
- 1 tsp minced cilantro
- 2 garlic cloves, minced
- 1 small sweet white onion, cut into ½ inch pieces
- 4-6 whole mini orange and red mini peppers
- ½ pineapple – save a few whole rings to grill
- 1 fresh lime, cut into wedges
- ⅓ cup melted butter or olive oil
- 1 tbsp fresh cilantro for garnish and butter
- Salt and pepper to taste
- Crushed red pepper – optional

Directions:
1. Preheat the grill to 400°F using direct heat with a cast iron grate installed.
2. In a large bowl, stir together the melted butter or olive oil, 1/3 cup orange juice, minced garlic, salt and pepper to taste. Squeeze a few wedges of the fresh lime juice into sauce and stir in 1 teaspoon minced cilantro. Set aside.
3. Thread chicken, onion, pineapple and whole mini peppers onto the skewers and brush with the cilantro lime butter marinade. Brush the pineapple rings with marinade and set aside.
4. Lightly oil the cooking grid. Grill the skewers for 8 to 12 minutes (turning so they don't burn) or until the internal temperature reaches 165°F. Remove from the kamado grill and grill the pineapple rings.
5. Plate and top with minced cilantro for garnish. If you like your food a bit spicier, sprinkle with crushed red pepper flakes.

Smoky Thai Pulled Chicken Sandwiches

Servings: 12
Cooking Time: 90 Minutes

Ingredients:

- 3 lbs boneless skinless chicken thighs
- 1 package of Cobblestone Bread Co.™ Sesame Twist Hamburger Rolls
- 3 tbs chopped cilantro
- quick pickled carrots
- * optional Sriracha sauce
- 3 cups water
- 2 tbs pure cane sugar
- juice of one lime
- 2 tsp Thai fish sauce
- 2 tsp soy sauce
- 1 tbs sea salt
- 1-2 hot peppers (Thai bird or Serrano)
- 2 cloves of garlic
- 1 tbs pure cane sugar
- 2 tsp sea salt
- 1 tsp onion powder
- ½ tsp ground ginger
- ½ tsp garlic powder
- ¼ tsp ground white pepper
- ¼ cup water
- ¼ cup honey
- 1 tbs fresh lime juice
- 2 tbs soy sauce
- 1 tsp Thai fish sauce (add while mixing, do not heat)
- ⅔ pound carrots
- 2½ cups water
- ⅔ cup rice wine vinegar
- 1 tbs pure cane sugar
- 2 tsp sea salt
- 2 tsp fresh grated ginger

Directions:

1. Whisk together ingredients for the brine. Add the chicken thighs, making sure they are fully covered. Place in refrigerator for 2-3 hours.
2. Preheat the grill to 280°F using direct heat with a cast iron grate installed.
3. Whisk together the dry rub ingredients. Remove the chicken thighs from brine, and pat dry. Discard brine. Generously coat the chicken with dry rub.
4. Place chicken thighs on the kamado grill. Cook for 1½ hours, flipping once after about 50 minutes. Check temperature occasionally to make sure you are not gout over a maximum of 325°F, damper more narrowly to reduce temperature closer to 280°F.
5. Prepare the Quick Pickled Carrots while the chicken is grilling.
6. When chicken thighs are removed from the kamado grill, set aside to rest and cool a little, then pull the chicken (discard any fatty bits). Mix in chopped fresh cilantro.
7. Mix sauce ingredients, except fish sauce, in a small saucepan over medium-high heat. Once it comes to a boil, reduce to a simmer. Allow to gently bubble for 2 minutes, then shut off and pour over the pulled chicken. Mix. Add fish sauce and mix again.

8. Place some of the pickled matchstick carrots on the bottom half of each Cobblestone Bread Co.™ Sesame Twist Hamburger Roll. Top with a generous helping of the Thai pulled chicken (squirt on a bit of sriracha sauce if you like) and cover with top of the roll.

9. Peel and trim carrots, then matchstick slice.

10. Whisk together pickling brine ingredients in a deep microwave-safe bowl. Microwave for 2 minutes, then whisk again to ensure salt & sugar are dissolved. Add the carrots. Make sure they are fully covered in the brine.

11. Microwave until the brine come to a quick boil (about 5-6 minutes). Microwave for another minute (you may need to stop it a couple times to avoid boil over). Remove from the microwave and set aside to cool.

12. When the brine has cooled to room temperature, drain. Refrigerate the carrots until ready to go on sandwiches.

Cuban Chicken Bombs

Servings: 4

Cooking Time: 30 Minutes

Ingredients:
- 4 bone in chicken thighs
- 4 slices of ham (cut into quarters)
- 4 slices of provolone (cut into quarters)
- 2 tbsp Dijon mustard
- 12 pickle chips
- 8 slices of bacon
- Sweet & Smoky Seasoning

Directions:
1. Preheat the grill to 300°F using direct heat with a cast iron grate installed.
2. Debone the chicken thighs leaving the skin on and position the chicken thighs skin side down. Spread equal portions of the mustard on the meat side of each chicken thigh. Place an equal amount of provolone slices, ham and pickles on each chicken thigh. Roll the chicken thighs up and wrap a piece of bacon around the middle of the chicken thigh and another around the thigh lengthwise sealing the contents with bacon. Put toothpicks through the bottom of the chicken thighs to help keep contents inside while cooking. Season the top of the bacon with the Sweet & Smokey Seasoning.
3. Cook the chicken for about an hour or until the internal temperature reaches 165°F. Remove the chicken from the kamado grill and let rest before slicing and serving.

Thai Stuffed Chicken Drumsticks

Servings: 10
Cooking Time: 40 Minutes

Ingredients:
- 3 lbs chicken drumsticks
- 1/2 lb ground pork
- 6 oz mushrooms, finely chopped
- 4 oz rice vermicelli noodles
- 2 Tablespoons fish sauce
- 1 Tablespoon freshly grated ginger
- 1 Tablespoon minced garlic (about 3 cloves)
- 2 tsp cornstarch
- 1 bunch green onions, finely chopped
- 1 egg
- 1 cup Thai sweet chili sauce
- 2 Tablespoons soy sauce
- 1 tsp fish sauce
- The juice of 1 lime

Directions:
1. Rinse and dry the drumsticks. Using your fingers, gently separate the skin from the meat beginning at the thickest part of the drumstick and leaving the skin attached at the bone.
2. In a large bowl, soak the vermicelli according to the package directions. When they are soft, cut into small pieces.
3. Mix noodles, ground pork, mushrooms, green onion, ginger, garlic, fish sauce, cornstarch, and egg. Divide into equal portions according to the number of drumsticks you intend to cook.
4. Gently work the stuffing under the skin of each drumstick.
5. Grilling:
6. Preheat the grill to 375°F using direct heat with a cast iron grate installed.
7. Place the drumsticks onto the grid and close the dome for 20 minutes.
8. Flip the drumsticks over and continue to cook an additional 20-25 minutes or until the skin is crispy and the juices of the chicken run clear.
9. Remove from the grid and mix ingredients for the dipping sauce. Serve.

Country Chicken Saltimbocca

Servings:8
Cooking Time: 30 Minutes

Ingredients:

- 3 6-8 oz (170-225 g) chicken breasts
- 4 cups (960 ml) cleaned and destemmed collard greens
- 6 slices cooked Applewood-smoked bacon, crumbled
- 2 tbsp (30 ml) extra virgin olive oil
- 2 cloves garlic, minced
- 3 slices aged cheddar cheese
- 1 tbsp (15 ml) garlic powder
- 1 tbsp (15 ml) onion powder
- 1 tsp (5 ml) white pepper
- 1 tbsp (15 ml) seasoning salt
- 4 tbsp (60 ml) butter
- 4 tbsp (60 ml) flour
- 2 cups (480 ml) half-and-half
- Reserved liquid from chicken
- 1 tbsp (15 ml) smoked paprika
- 6 leaves of basil

Directions:

1. Preheat the grill to 350°F using direct heat with a cast iron grate installed.
2. Pound chicken breasts until ¼ inch thick. Coat chicken breasts with ¾ of the seasoning mix; set aside.
3. Chiffonade collard greens into strips no wider than ¼ inch. Heat a Cast Iron Skillet with the olive oil. Add greens, then garlic and the remaining seasoning mix, cooking until wilted, 5-7 minutes.
4. Lay out the chicken breasts with the interior side up. Layer each in the following order: one slice of cheese, 1/3 of the bacon crumbles, 1/3 of the cooked collards. The bacon and collards should be placed in a thin even layer across the whole breast. Beginning at the short tapered end, roll up each chicken breast as you would for a jellyroll. Secure with a toothpick.
5. Place rolls in a Roasting & Drip Pan, evenly spaced with room between each roll.
6. Place the pan on the grid and bake for 15 to 20 minutes or until the chicken is firm. Remove from the kamado grill and allow to rest for at least 5 minutes. Remove the chicken from the pan; reserve the liquid for the sauce.
7. Remove the platesetter and grill each side of the chicken for 1 minute for color and added flavor. Gently slice each into pinwheels, no less than ½ inch wide. Top with sauce and serve.
8. Mix all seasoning ingredients together and set aside.
9. Melt butter in a sauce pan. Whisk flour into butter. Cook for 90 seconds once incorporated, continuously whisking. Slowly add half-and-half, whisking in each addition until incorporated in flour mix. Season to taste. Add the reserved chicken liquid the same way. Add smoked paprika and cook at a low simmer for 2 minutes, or until it's at the thickness you desire; remove from heat. Chiffonade basil, add to warm sauce just before serving.

Brined Roasted Turkey

Servings: 4

Cooking Time: 240 Minutes

Ingredients:

- 4 qts water
- 1 ½ cup kosher salt
- ½ cup sugar
- 2 bay leaves
- 2 tbsp black peppercorns
- 1 tbsp dried sage
- 1 orange, cut in half
- 1 lemon, cut in half
- 1 onion, cut in half
- 8 cloves of garlic
- Enough ice to fill the bottom of the brining bucket about 3 inches
- 1 12-14 lb. whole turkey
- 1 orange, cut into wedges
- 1 sweet onion, cut into wedges
- 1 lemon, cut into wedges
- 2 whole heads of garlic, top cut off
- 3 sprigs rosemary
- 3 sprigs thyme
- 3 sprigs sage
- Savory Pecan Seasoning
- Extra virgin olive oil or canola oil
- Kosher salt

Directions:

1. A day before your cook, put all the brine ingredients, except for ice, into a pot and boil for 10 minutes. Pour liquid over ice into the brining bucket. Once the liquid is cool place the turkey into the bucket, making sure the turkey is completely submerged. Cover tightly, and put into the fridge and brine for 8-24 hours. When ready to cook, remove the turkey from the brine and rinse thoroughly.
2. Preheat the grill to 350°F using direct heat with a cast iron grate installed.
3. Pat the turkey dry and coat with oil, season with salt and Savory Pecan Seasoning.
4. Place half of the onion, one whole head of garlic, half the orange, half the lemon, and two sprigs of each herb inside the cavity of the turkey. Fold the wings back behind the turkey so that they cook evenly. Put the turkey on the roasting rack and place into the drip pan. Add the remaining garlic, onion, orange, lemon and herbs around the turkey in the drip pan.
5. Place on the kamado grill and cook 3-4 hours or until the internal temperature is 165°F (white meat) and 185°F (dark meat). During the cook, cover the turkey with aluminum foil once the skin has the desired color and texture.
6. Remove from the kamado grill, let rest for 15 minutes. Carve and enjoy!

Spicy Bourbon Barrel Bbq Wings

Servings:12

Cooking Time: 150 Minutes

Ingredients:

- 3 dozen Springer Mountain Farms Chicken Wings
- 1 liter bourbon
- 4 cups brown sugar
- 1 yellow onion, chopped
- 2 cups dark molasses
- 1 quart ketchup
- 1 cup Worcestershire Sauce
- ½ cup whole fresh garlic
- ½ cup chopped chipotle peppers
- 1 whole bunch, not chopped thyme
- 3 tablespoon Liquid Smoke
- 1 cup honey
- 2 cups Dijon mustard
- 2 oranges, cut in quarters
- Salt to taste

Directions:

1. Combine all ingredients for the sauce in a large stock box and let simmer on low heat for 2 hours, then remove oranges, thyme, and onions. Blend the sauce until smooth, then pour through a strainer. Toss the chicken in the sauce and drain extra sauce.

2. Preheat the grill to 375°F using direct heat with a cast iron grate installed. Cook for about 30 minutes, turning occasionally, until the internal temperature reaches 165°F or higher.

Peking Duck

Servings: 6
Cooking Time: 250 Minutes

Ingredients:
- 1 (5 lb) duck
- 1/4 cup Asian Rub
- 1 cup Chinese Barbecue Sauce (optional)

Directions:
1. Pat the duck dry.
2. Score the duck skin in one direction, then the other so you end up with a diamond pattern on the skin. (Scoring means you only cut through the skin, not the fat or meat.)
3. Liberally season all sides and the cavity with Asian Rub.
4. Allow the duck to rest in the fridge for 1 hour, bringing it back to room temperature while the grill preheats.
5. Grilling:
6. Preheat the grill to 300°F using direct heat with a cast iron grate installed, placing the plate setter and grids inside.
7. Place the duck, breast side up, on a rack, in a roasting pan that will fit inside the grill. The duck will render about 1 1/2 cups of fat.
8. Place the roasting rack inside the grill and close the dome for 1 hour.
9. Flip the duck back side up and close the dome for 1 hour.
10. Flip the duck breast side up and close the dome for 1 hour.
11. Finally, flip the duck back side up and close the dome for 1 hour.
12. Baste the duck with Chinese Barbecue Sauce (if desired). Adjust the temperature to 400°F. Close the dome for a final 5-7 minutes to crisp the skin, and remove.
13. Allow to sit uncovered for 10 minutes before carving.
14. Substitute duck fat for olive oil when cooking potatoes, root vegetables, or even eggs. Once rendered, strain the fat of any solids and save it in an airtight container in the fridge for up to 1 week.

Smoked Turkey

Servings: 8
Cooking Time: 38minutes

Ingredients:
- 12-14 lb. whole turkey
- Sweet and Smoky Seasoning
- Canola oil
- Kosher salt
- ½ orange, cut in half
- ½ onion, cut in half
- 2 sprigs sage
- 2 sprigs rosemary
- 2 sprigs thyme
- 1 whole head of garlic

Directions:
1. Preheat the grill to 225°F using direct heat with a cast iron grate installed.
2. Coat the turkey in canola oil and place on rib rack inside of the roasting pan. Season with salt and sweet and smoky seasoning making sure to season the cavity as well. Put orange, onion, garlic and herbs into the cavity.
3. Smoke in the kamado grill until the internal temperature of the breast meat is 165ºF, the dark meat will be about 185ºF internal temperature. Typically, it is about 30 minutes per lb., between 6 to 8 hours.
4. Let rest for 15 minutes, and serve!

Smoked Curried Chicken Salad With Grilled Naan Bread

Servings: 8

Cooking Time: 45 Minutes

Ingredients:
- 1 lb. boneless chicken breasts
- 2-3 slices of naan bread
- 2 tbsp of mayonnaise or plain Greek yogurt
- ½ small red onion, chopped
- 2 green onions, chopped
- ½ small red and green bell pepper or 2 whole mini red and green sweet peppers, chopped
- ⅓ cup chopped fresh celery
- Spring mix or other tender salad greens
- Ground black pepper
- Coarse salt
- Coarse salt to taste
- 1 tsp ground coriander seeds
- 1½ tsp cumin
- 1 tbsp course black pepper
- ½ tsp ground ginger
- 1 tbsp dried basil
- 1 tbsp garlic powder
- 1 tbsp dried lime zest
- 1 tsp ground turmeric
- 1 tsp – or to taste, hot red chilis, crushed red pepper flakes cayenne or Thai bird chili powder
- Olive oil to brush onto chicken

Directions:
1. Preheat the grill to 250°F using direct heat with a cast iron grate installed.
2. Season the chicken breasts with green curry rub, brush lightly with olive oil. Place directly on the cast iron grid and smoke for 45 minutes or until internal temperature reaches 165°F. Remove from the kamado grill and let rest. Brush naan bread with olive oil and grill.
3. Cut the smoked chicken breasts into bite-size pieces and mix with the mayonnaise or Greek yogurt, red onion, green onions, red and green bell peppers, celery, salt and pepper. Combine the mixture well and serve over mixed greens. Salt and pepper to taste.
4. For the green curry rub, mix all ingredients together in a small bowl. You can make this as spicy as you wish by adding more chili powder and or crushed red pepper flakes.

DESSERTS

Orange Scented Vanilla Cake

Servings: 12
Cooking Time: 30 Minutes

Ingredients:
- 12 oranges
- 1/2 stick of butter
- 1 vanilla cake mix, prepared according to package instructions
- 1/2 lb of powdered sugar

Directions:
1. Cut the tops off of the oranges and, using a spoon, scoop out the insides of the orange. Eat the insides of the orange while you wait for the cake to cook.
2. Pour 1/3 of a cup of batter into each orange, replace the top and wrap with heavy duty aluminum foil.
3. In a separate bowl, combine butter, powdered sugar, and 2 Tablespoon orange juice.
4. When cakes are ready, drizzle some of the glaze over top of each cake and serve inside the orange.
5. Grilling:
6. Place the oranges on a 350°F grill for 30 minutes or until the cake is done.

Sourdough Baguette

Servings: 4
Cooking Time: 25 Minutes

Ingredients:

- cornmeal, for dusting
- for Day 1 (starter)
- 8oz (225g) whole rye flour
- 8oz (235ml) warm water (105°F [41°C])
- for Day 2
- 8oz (225g) bread flour
- for Day 3
- 12oz (340g) bread flour
- 6oz (177ml) warm water (105°F [41°C])
- 8oz (225g) starter
- for Day 4
- 3oz (85g) whole rye flour
- 31oz (915ml) warm water (105°F [41°C])
- 9 1/2 oz (270g) starter
- 42oz (1.2kg) bread flour
- 3oz (85g) whole wheat flour
- 1oz (25g) kosher salt

Directions:

1. On Day 1, in a large bowl, combine flour and water, cover tightly with plastic wrap, and let sit overnight on the counter at warm room temperature, about 70°F (21°C). (Cooler temperatures might inhibit the growth of the starter.)
2. On Day 2, add flour to the starter and mix until a stiff, thick dough forms. Cover tightly with plastic wrap and let sit overnight on the counter at warm room temperature. The dough will rise overnight.
3. On Day 3, in a large bowl, combine flour, water, and 8 ounces (225g) of the starter, and mix until a stiff, thick dough forms. Cover tightly with plastic wrap and let sit overnight on the counter at warm room temperature. The dough will rise overnight and should begin to smell yeasty. (Freeze remaining starter for later use.)
4. On Day 4, preheat the grill to 400°F (204°C) using indirect heat with a standard grate installed and a pizza stone on the grate. In a large bowl, combine rye flour, water, 9 1/2 ounces (270g) of the starter, bread flour, wheat flour, and salt, and mix until a dough forms. Cover tightly with plastic wrap and let sit for 20 minutes on the counter. The dough will continue to smell yeasty. (Freeze remaining starter for later use.)
5. Form the dough into 4 baguette shapes that are 10 to 12 inches (25cm to 30.5cm) long and about 2 1/2 inches (6.25cm) around. Make 3 slits in the top of each loaf to allow steam to escape. Sprinkle the pizza stone with cornmeal and place the loaves on the pizza stone. Close the lid and bake until the bread reaches an internal temperature of 190°F (88°C), about 20 to 25 minutes.
6. Remove the baguettes from the grill, place on a cutting board, and let rest before slicing and serving as desired.

3 Ingredient Fruit Cobbler

Servings: 8
Cooking Time: 30 Minutes

Ingredients:
- 1 stick butter, sliced
- 2 (29 oz) cans fruit, drained but reserving 1/2 cup of the liquid
- 1 yellow cake mix

Directions:
1. Line the dutch oven with a liner
2. Pour fruit into the bottom of the dutch oven with 1/2 cup of reserved liquid
3. Sprinkle the top with cake mix
4. Dot the top with butter.
5. Grilling:
6. Preheat the grill to 350°F using direct heat with a cast iron grate installed.
7. Cover the dutch oven and place on the grid of the grill.
8. Lower the dome for 30 minutes.
9. Allow the cobbler to sit for 10 minutes off the heat before serving.

Almond Cream Cake

Servings: 16
Cooking Time: 45 Minutes

Ingredients:

- 2 cups butter, softened
- 3 cups sugar
- 6 cups cake flour
- 1 tsp kosher salt
- 4 tsp baking powder
- 2 cups whole milk
- 2 tsp almond extract
- 10 large eggs, whites only
- sliced almonds, to decorate
- for the frosting
- 1 1/4 cups all-purpose flour
- 2 cups whole milk
- 1/2 tsp almond extract
- 1 tbsp vanilla bean paste
- 2 cups butter, softened
- 2 cups sugar

Directions:

1. In the bowl of a stand mixer fitted with the paddle attachment, cream butter until white in appearance. Add sugar and beat until fluffy. In a large bowl, sift together flour, salt, and baking powder. Add the flour mixture to the butter mixture in three stages, alternating with the milk and almond extract and mixing after each addition until just combined.

2. In a large bowl, beat egg whites until they form stiff peaks. Using a spatula, gently fold egg whites into the cake batter, taking care not to overmix.

3. Preheat the grill to 350°F (177°C) using indirect heat with a standard grate installed. Line an 11 x 18-in (28 x 46cm) grill-safe baking pan with parchment paper and lightly grease with cooking spray. Pour the batter into the pan, place on the grate, close the lid, and bake until the top springs back when touched, about 27 to 30 minutes.

4. Remove the cake from the grill and place on a wire rack to cool for 10 minutes. Use a knife to loosen the edges, and transfer the cake to a wire rack to cool completely.

5. To make the frosting, on the stovetop in a saucepan over medium-low heat, whisk together flour and milk until mixture thickens to the consistency of mashed potatoes, about 12 to 15 minutes. Stir constantly, and lower the heat if needed. Remove the saucepan from the heat and place in a bowl of ice for 5 to 10 minutes to hasten the cooling process and bring the mixture to room temperature. Once cool, stir in almond extract.

6. In the bowl of a stand mixer, cream together vanilla paste, butter, and sugar until the mixture is light and fluffy and sugar is completely dissolved. Add the flour mixture, and beat until it has the appearance of whipped cream, scraping the sides of the bowl as needed.

7. Spread the frosting evenly over the cooled cake and sprinkle sliced almonds over top to decorate before serving.

Buttermilk Biscuits

Servings: 6
Cooking Time: 15 Minutes

Ingredients:
- 3/4 cups buttermilk
- 1/2 cup butter, cut into 1/2 inch cubes
- 3 cups flour
- 1 1/2 tsp baking powder
- 1/2 tsp salt

Directions:
1. In the bowl of a food processor, combine flour, baking powder, salt and butter and pulse until the butter is the size of small peas.
2. With the food processor going, stream in buttermilk until the dough just comes together.
3. Turn out on a floured surface.
4. Pat the dough to 1/2-inch thickness and fold in half.
5. Pat the dough to 1/2-inch thickness and fold in half again.
6. Pat the dough a third time to 1/2-inch thickness.
7. Using a pizza cutter, cut the dough into 12 square biscuits.
8. Place a sheet of parchment in the bottom of the dutch oven.
9. Place biscuits on the bottom of the dutch oven, being careful that they do not touch. (You may have to do this in two batches.)
10. Grilling:
11. Preheat the grill to 425°F using direct heat with a cast iron grate installed.
12. Cover the dutch oven with the lid and place on the grid.
13. Lower the dome for 12-15 minutes.
14. Biscuits are done when they are golden brown. Serve with butter, honey, or jam.

Fresh Peach Crisp

Servings: 4
Cooking Time: 5 Minutes

Ingredients:
- 2 peaches, halved with pits removed
- Vanilla Ice Cream
- 1 cup good quality granola

Directions:
1. Grilling:
2. Place the peach halves, cut side down, on a 400°F grill and cover with the dome for 5 minutes.
3. Assembly:
4. Remove the peaches and place them, cut side up, in a bowl. Top with vanilla ice cream and granola.

Grilled Naan

Servings: 24
Cooking Time: 6 Minutes

Ingredients:

- 1 cup warm water (105°F [41°C])
- 1/4oz (7g) active dry yeast
- 1/4 cup sugar
- 3 tbsp whole milk
- 1 large egg, beaten
- 2 tsp kosher salt
- 20 1/4oz (575g) bread flour, plus more for kneading
- vegetable oil, for greasing
- 1/4 cup butter, melted

Directions:

1. In a large bowl, combine water and yeast. Let sit until frothy, about 10 minutes. Stir in sugar, milk, egg, salt, and flour to make a soft dough. Knead on a lightly floured surface until smooth.
2. Lightly oil a large bowl, place the dough in the bowl, and cover with a damp cloth. Let sit to rise until the dough has doubled in volume, about 1 hour.
3. Punch the dough down and divide it into 4 balls (about the size of golf balls). Cover with a towel and allow to rise until the balls have doubled in size, about 30 minutes.
4. Preheat the grill to 425°F (218°C) using direct heat with a cast iron grate installed. Use a rolling pin one ball of dough into a thin circle. Lightly oil the grate, place the circle of dough on the grate, close the lid, and bake until puffy and lightly browned, about 2 to 3 minutes. Brush the uncooked side with butter, then flip the dough over and brush the cooked side with butter. Cook until puffy and lightly browned, about 3 minutes more. Repeat the cooking process with the remaining dough. (You can also bake all 4 balls at the same time.)
5. Remove the naan from the grill and sprinkle with seasoning of choice (if desired). Serve warm.

Grilled Pineapple Sundaes

Servings: 4
Cooking Time: 5 Minutes

Ingredients:

- 4 fresh pineapple spears
- Vanilla Ice Cream
- Jarred Caramel Sauce
- Toasted Coconut

Directions:

1. Place pineapple spears on a 400°F grill and close the dome for 2 minutes.
2. Turn the pineapple and close the dome for another 2 minutes.
3. Turn the pineapple once more and close the dome for another minute.
4. Assembly:
5. Serve pineapple topped with ice cream, caramel sauce, and toasted coconut.

4 Ingredient, No Knead Bread

Servings: 4
Cooking Time: 30 Minutes

Ingredients:
- 3 cups warm water
- 1 1/2 Tablespoons yeast
- 1 1/2 Tablespoons salt
- 6 1/2 cups bread flour

Directions:
1. In a 4-quart ice cream container, mix all ingredients until they come together. DO NOT KNEAD.
2. Cover, but do not seal the container and allow it to sit in a warm, dry place until it doubles in size, about 30 minutes.
3. Seal the container and place in the fridge for 1 hour.
4. Place a sheet of parchment paper in the bottom of the dutch oven.
5. Pinch off 1/4 of the dough and form into a ball.
6. Place the ball on the parchment paper and allow it to rest while the grill heats.
7. Grilling:
8. Preheat the grill to 425°F using direct heat with a cast iron grate installed.
9. Score the top of the dough ball with an "X".
10. Cover the dutch oven and place it on the grid of the grill.
11. Lower the Dome for 30 minutes.
12. Remove the bread from the dutch oven and allow it to cool before slicing.

Seasonal Fruit Cobbler

Servings: 12
Cooking Time: 90 Minutes

Ingredients:
- 2lb (1kg) seasonal fruit, washed, pitted (if needed), and sliced or halved if needed
- 1/2 tsp ground cinnamon
- 2 tsp cornstarch (for juicy fruits; omit for pears or apples)
- 4 tbsp butter, plus more for greasing
- 1/2 cup sugar, plus more for sprinkling
- 3/4 cup self-rising flour
- 3/4 cup whole milk
- whipped cream, to serve

Directions:
1. Preheat the grill to 350°F (177°C) using indirect heat with a standard grate installed. Place the fruit on the grate (or in a cast iron skillet if the fruit might fall through the grate), close the lid, and grill until beginning to soften and char, about 7 to 10 minutes. Remove fruit from the grill and place in a large bowl. Sprinkle cinnamon and cornstarch (if using) over fruit, and add a little sugar (if desired). Gently toss to coat and set aside.
2. Grease a 9-in (23-cm) grill-safe baking pan with butter. On the stovetop in a small saucepan, heat 4 tbsp butter over medium-low heat until beginning to brown, about 10 to 15 minutes.
3. In a medium bowl, whisk together butter, sugar, flour, and milk. Transfer fruit to the prepared baking pan and spread the batter evenly over top. Place the pan on the grate, close the lid, and bake until golden brown and bubbly, about 1 hour. In the last 10 minutes of cooking, sprinkle a light amount of sugar over top. Remove the cobbler from the grill, and serve warm with whipped cream on top.

Nutella And Strawberry Pizza

Servings: 8
Cooking Time: 5 Minutes

Ingredients:
- 1 pizza dough
- 1/2 lb sliced strawberries
- 1/4 cup Nutella

Directions:
1. Stretch the pizza dough into a 14 inch round and place it on a pizza peel.
2. Spread the dough with the Nutella and top with strawberries.
3. Grilling:
4. Slide the pizza onto the prepared stone in a 500°F grill and cook for 5 minutes.
5. Remove from the stone with a pizza peel and slice into 8 pieces.

S'mores Pizza

Servings: 8
Cooking Time: 5 Minutes

Ingredients:
- 1 pizza dough
- 1/2 cup semi-sweet chocolate chips
- 1/2 cup miniature marshmallows
- 1/4 cup slightly crushed graham crackers

Directions:
1. Stretch dough to a 14" round and place on a pizza peel.
2. Sprinkle dough with chocolate chips, miniature marshmallows, and graham cracker crumbs.
3. Grilling:
4. Slide the pizza onto the prepared stone at 500°F.
5. Cook for 5 minutes, remove from the stone, slice, and serve.

Chocolate Cake

Servings: 12
Cooking Time: 45 Minutes

Ingredients:

- 2 cups all-purpose flour
- 2 cups sugar
- 2/3 cup cocoa powder
- 2 tsp baking soda
- 1 tsp baking powder
- 1 tsp kosher salt
- 2 large eggs, at room temperature
- 1 cup buttermilk, at room temperature
- 1 cup strong black coffee, warm
- 1/2 cup vegetable oil
- 1 tbsp pure vanilla extract
- flaky sea salt, for topping (optional)
- for the caramel sauce
- 3/4 cup sugar
- 4 tbsp water
- 4 tsp light corn syrup
- 1/4 cup heavy cream
- 1 tsp pure vanilla extract
- 1 1/2 tbsp unsalted butter
- for the frosting
- 12 tbsp unsalted butter, at room temperature
- 2 1/2 cups powdered sugar
- 1 tsp pure vanilla extract
- 1 tbsp heavy cream
- kosher salt

Directions:

1. Preheat the grill to 350°F (177°C) using indirect heat with a standard grate installed. Grease a 9-in (23-cm) round metal cake pan with nonstick cooking spray and line with parchment paper. (Instead of a cake pan, you can also use a well-seasoned dutch oven.)

2. In a large bowl or the bowl of a stand mixer, sift together flour, sugar, cocoa powder, baking soda, baking powder, and salt. In a separate medium bowl, whisk together eggs, buttermilk, coffee, vegetable oil, and vanilla extract.

3. Gradually add the liquid ingredients to the dry ingredients, stopping to scrape the sides and bottom of the bowl, until just combined. (The batter will be thin.) Pour the batter into the prepared cake pan or dutch oven. Place on the grate, close the grill lid, and bake until a toothpick inserted in the center comes out almost clean, about 25 to 30 minutes. Let sit for 5 minutes, then turn out onto a wire rack to cool completely. (Use a butter knife to loosen the edges if needed.)

4. To make the caramel sauce, in a small saucepan, combine sugar, water, and corn syrup. Place on the stovetop over medium heat, and simmer until the mixture is deep amber in color, about 10 to 15 minutes. Slowly and carefully, add heavy cream, whisking constantly, then whisk in vanilla, butter, and a pinch of salt.

5. To make the frosting, in the bowl of a stand mixer fitted with the paddle attachment, beat butter on medium speed until light and fluffy, about 2 to 3 minutes. Add sugar, vanilla extract, heavy cream, and a pinch of salt. Beat on low speed until combined, about 1 minute. Increase the speed to medium-high and beat for 6 minutes. Add 1/2 cup caramel sauce and mix until combined.

6. Spread the frosting evenly over top and sides of the cooled cake, and drizzle with caramel sauce. Sprinkle with flaky sea salt (if desired) before serving.

Bread Pudding

Servings: 8
Cooking Time: 60 Minutes

Ingredients:

- 1 1/2 cups milk
- 10 eggs
- 1 loaf French bread, cut into 1 1/2 inch cubes
- 1 1/2 cups sugar
- 1 cup raisins (optional)
- 2 Tablespoons vanilla
- 2 tsp cinnamon
- 1/2 tsp nutmeg
- 1/4 tsp salt

Directions:

1. Line the dutch oven with a liner.
2. Place bread cubes and raisins into the dutch oven.
3. In a large bowl, combine eggs, milk, sugar, vanilla, cinnamon, nutmeg, and salt.
4. Pour the mixture over the bread and raisins.
5. Allow the bread mixture to sit for 30 minutes.
6. Grilling:
7. Preheat the grill to 350°F using direct heat with a cast iron grate installed.
8. Cover the dutch oven, place it on the grid, and lower the dome for 1 hour.
9. Serve the bread pudding with vanilla ice cream or whipped cream.

Grilled Sopapillas

Servings: 6
Cooking Time: 18 Minutes

Ingredients:

- 1 pizza dough, divided into 6 pieces
- 3 Tablespoons melted butter
- 1/4 cup sugar
- 1 Tablespoon cinnamon

Directions:

1. Stretch dough into round shape.
2. Place the dough directly on the pizza stone in a 500°F grill.
3. Brush with melted butter and top with cinnamon sugar.
4. Close the dome for 3 minutes, then remove.
5. Repeat with remaining dough.

Lemon Poppy Seed Cake

Servings: 10
Cooking Time: 45 Minutes

Ingredients:

- 1 tsp poppy seeds
- 2 lemons, zested and juiced
- 1 vanilla cake mix prepared according to package directions, substituting melted butter for oil and buttermilk for water
- 1 lb powdered sugar
- 4 ounces cream cheese
- 1 stick butter, softened
- 1/2 tsp vanilla
- 1/2 tsp lemon extract
- The juice and zest of 1 lemon

Directions:

1. Prepare cake mix according to package directions, substituting melted butter for the oil and buttermilk for the water.
2. Add the lemon zest, lemon juice, and poppy seeds.
3. Line the dutch oven with a liner.
4. Pour prepare cake mix into the liner and cover.
5. Grilling:
6. Preheat the grill to 350°F using direct heat with a cast iron grate installed.
7. Place the dutch oven on the grid and lower the dome for 30-40 minutes or until a toothpick inserted into the center comes out clean.
8. Meanwhile, combine glaze ingredients, adding milk to thin out the glaze if necessary.
9. Remove the cake from the grill and set aside to cool for 10 minutes before pouring glaze over the cake.
10. Serve warm.

Banana Boats

Servings: 4
Cooking Time: 10 Minutes

Ingredients:

- 4 green bananas
- Chocolate chips
- Miniature marshmallows
- Peanut butter chips
- Crushed cookies

Directions:

1. Split a banana lengthwise from end to end leaving the peel intact on the opposite side.
2. Top with desired toppings.
3. Wrap the banana in heavy duty aluminum foil.
4. Grilling:
5. Preheat the grill to 425°F using direct heat with a cast iron grate installed and close the dome for 10 minutes.
6. Unwrap and serve topped with vanilla ice cream, whipped cream, or by themselves

Peach Dutch Baby

Servings: 8

Cooking Time: 25 Minutes

Ingredients:
- 8 oz frozen peaches, thawed (or 3 ripe peaches, peeled and sliced)
- 1 cup whole milk
- 4 eggs
- 1 cup flour
- 1/4 cup sugar
- 1/4 cup butter
- 1 tsp vanilla
- 1 tsp cinnamon
- 1/2 tsp salt

Directions:
1. In a blender, combine milk, flour, sugar, vanilla, cinnamon, salt, and eggs until smooth.
2. Grilling:
3. Preheat the grill to 425°F using direct heat with a cast iron grate installed.
4. Place the dutch oven on the grid of the grill and melt the butter.
5. Line the bottom of the pot with peaches and pour over milk and egg mixture.
6. Close the dome for 20 minutes or until the top of the Dutch Baby is golden brown.
7. Serve with a sprinkling of powdered sugar.

Berry Upside-down Cake

Servings: 10
Cooking Time: 30 Minutes

Ingredients:
- 10 tbsp unsalted butter, at room temperature, divided
- 1 cup packed light brown sugar, divided
- 11oz (315g) fresh seasonal berries
- 1 large egg
- 1 tsp pure vanilla extract
- 2/3 cup sour cream
- 1 1/3 cups all-purpose flour
- 1 tbsp baking powder
- 1/4 tsp baking soda
- 1/2 tsp kosher salt
- 1/4 tsp ground cinnamon
- fresh mint leaves, to garnish
- whipped cream, to serve

Directions:
1. Preheat the grill to 350°F (177°C) using indirect heat with a standard grate installed and a cast iron skillet on the grate. Melt 2 tbsp butter in the skillet and swirl to coat. Remove the skillet from the grill. Sprinkle 1/3 cup brown sugar over butter, pour in berries, and shake the skillet until berries are evenly spread out. Set aside.
2. In the bowl of a stand mixer fitted with the paddle attachment, cream together remaining 8 tbsp butter and 2/3 cup brown sugar until fluffy. Add egg, vanilla, and sour cream, and beat to combine.
3. In a medium bowl, sift together flour, baking powder, baking soda, salt, and cinnamon. Gradually add the dry ingredients to the butter and egg mixture until just incorporated. (The batter will be thick.) Using a rubber spatula, scoop the batter into the skillet, smoothing it over berries.
4. Place the skillet on the grate, close the lid, and bake until golden brown and a cake tester inserted into the middle of the cake comes out clean, about 30 minutes. Remove the skillet from the grill and place on a wire rack to cool for 15 minutes.
5. To serve, flip the cake upside down on a large serving platter and release from the skillet, leaving the berries on top. Garnish with fresh mint leaves, and serve with a dollop of whipped cream.

Apple Cake

Servings: 12
Cooking Time: 60 Minutes

Ingredients:
- 2 (21 oz) cans apple pie filling
- 1 (14 oz) jar caramel ice cream topping
- 1 box yellow cake mix, prepared according to package directions and mixed with 2 tsp cinnamon

Directions:
1. Prepare cake according to package directions.
2. Line a dutch oven with a liner.
3. Pour pie filling into the bottom of the dutch oven.
4. Top with caramel ice cream topping.
5. Top with prepared cake mix.
6. Grilling:
7. Preheat the grill to 350°F using direct heat with a cast iron grate installed.
8. Cover the dutch oven and place on the grid of the grill.
9. Lower the dome and cook for 1 hour.
10. Serve warm with whipped cream or ice cream.

Grilled Fruit Pie

Servings: 8
Cooking Time: 55 Minutes

Ingredients:
- for the crust
- 1 cup all-purpose flour, plus extra for rolling dough
- 1/2 tsp kosher salt
- 1/2 cup butter, chilled and cut into small cubes
- 1/4 cup ice water
- 2lb (1kg) dried beans, for blind baking
- powdered sugar, for dusting
- whipped cream or ice cream, to serve (optional)
- for the filling
- 1 1/4lb (565g) seasonal fruit, such as pears and plums, halved and pitted
- 1/2 cup sugar
- 4 tbsp cornstarch
- 2 tbsp lemon juice

Directions:
1. Preheat the grill to 350°F (177°C) using indirect heat with a standard grate installed. Place fruit on the grate skin side up, keeping them toward the edges of the grate. Close the lid and grill until beginning to soften, about 3 to 5 minutes. Transfer to a cutting board and slice. Set aside.
2. To make the crust, in a food processor, combine flour and salt, pulsing 3 to 4 times. Add butter, and pulse until the texture is mealy, about 5 to 6 times. With the food processor running, slowly add the ice water in 1 tbsp increments until the dough comes together.
3. Turn out the dough onto a floured work surface and sprinkle with flour. Using a rolling pin, roll dough out to a 10- to 11-in (25- to 28-cm) circle. Carefully transfer the dough to a 9-in (23-cm) metal pie pan, pressing the dough to the edges. Trim any overhang and crimp the edges. Prick the dough with a fork to prevent bubbles during baking. Place the pan in the fridge to chill for 15 minutes.
4. Spread a large piece of parchment paper over the dough and fill the pan with dry beans, pressing them into the edges of the dough. Place the pan on the grate, close the lid, and bake for 10 minutes. Remove the parchment and beans from the pan, and continue baking the crust until golden brown in color, about 10 to 15 minutes more. Remove the pan from the grill and let the crust cool completely before filling.
5. To make the filling, in a large bowl, combine sugar, cornstarch, and juice. Add the grilled fruit and toss lightly to coat. Pour the fruit mixture into the baked crust. Place on the grate, close the lid, and bake until the filling is thickened and bubbling at the edges, about 30 minutes.
6. Remove the pie from the grill and place on a wire rack to cool. Just before serving, sprinkle with powdered sugar. Serve with whipped cream or ice cream (if desired).

Death By Chocolate

Servings: 8
Cooking Time: 60 Minutes

Ingredients:
- 1 chocolate cake mix, prepared according to package directions
- 2 cups chocolate chips
- 1 cup brown sugar
- 1 1/2 cups water
- 1/2 cup cocoa powder
- 1 (10 oz) bag miniature marshmallows

Directions:
1. Prepare cake mix according to package instructions.
2. Line the dutch oven with a liner.
3. In a medium bowl, combine water, brown sugar, and cocoa powder.
4. Pour the mixture into the bottom of the dutch oven.
5. Top with miniature marshmallows
6. Pour prepared cake mix on top.
7. Top with chocolate chips.
8. Grilling:
9. Preheat the grill to 350°F using direct heat with a cast iron grate installed.
10. Place the lid on the dutch oven and set on the grid of the grill.
11. Close the dome for 1 hour.
12. Remove the dutch oven from the grill, uncover, and serve warm.

Chocolate Chip Cookie Peanut Butter Cup S'mores

Servings: 4
Cooking Time: 5 Minutes

Ingredients:
- 8 chocolate chip cookies
- 4 peanut butter cup candies
- 4 marshmallows

Directions:
1. On the grid of a 225°F grill, place one cookie, flat side up, with one peanut butter cup candy and one marshmallow on top.
2. Close the dome for 5 minutes or until the marshmallow begins to puff.
3. Assembly:
4. Close the s'more with the other chocolate chip cookie and get ready for the sugar rush.

Best Banana Bread

Servings: 6
Cooking Time: 40 Minutes

Ingredients:

- 1 cup plain yogurt
- 1/4 cup butter
- 3 very ripe bananas, peeled
- 2 eggs
- 2 cups flour
- 2/3 cups sugar
- 3/4 tsp salt
- 1/2 tsp vanilla extract
- 1/2 tsp baking soda
- 1/4 tsp baking powder

Directions:

1. In a blender, combine bananas, yogurt, sugar, butter, vanilla, and eggs until smooth.
2. In a large bowl, sift together flour, salt, baking powder, and baking soda.
3. Gradually add the wet ingredients into the dry ingredients and gently stir to combine. DO NOT OVER MIX.
4. Line a dutch oven with a liner.
5. Pour batter into the dutch oven and cover.
6. Grilling:
7. Preheat the grill to 350°F using direct heat with a cast iron grate installed and place the dutch oven on the grid.
8. Lower the dome for 30 minutes or until a toothpick inserted into the center comes out clean.

Peaches And Pound Cake

Servings: 6
Cooking Time: 5 Minutes

Ingredients:

- 1/2 cup heavy whipping cream
- 2 Tablespoons sour cream
- 3 peaches, halved and pitted
- 1 store-bought pound cake, cut into 6 slices

Directions:

1. Place the peaches, cut side down, on a 400°F grill.
2. Place the pound cake slices alongside the peaches and close the dome for 2 minutes.
3. Flip the pound cake, and close the dome for an additional 2-3 minutes.
4. Assembly:
5. In a stand mixer, whip the whipping cream until stiff peaks form. Fold in the sour cream to combine.
6. Place a slice of pound cake on a plate, top with a peach half, and a dollop of the cream.

BEEF

Grilled Veal Chop With Fresh Herbs

Servings: 4
Cooking Time: 12 Minutes

Ingredients:
- Bone-in veal chop, 1½ - 2 inches thick
- Kosher salt
- Fresh ground pepper
- 6-10 fresh basil leaves, chopped
- A small bunch fresh parsley, chopped
- 4-6 leaves fresh sage, chopped
- 1 sprig fresh rosemary, chopped
- 3 garlic cloves, chopped
- ½ cup extra virgin olive oil, separated

Directions:
1. Preheat the grill to 500°F using direct heat with a cast iron grate installed.
2. Drizzle ¼ cup of olive oil and season veal chop with kosher salt and ground pepper and let it rest for 20 to 30 minutes.
3. Mix together the fresh ingredients, salt, pepper and ¼ cup of olive oil (more if necessary, to ensure the herbs are covered). Let the mixture rest to mend the flavors together.
4. Cook the veal chop for approximately 4-6 mins per side, until the internal temperature is between 135°F and 140°F. Remove from the kamado grill and baste the chop with the herb mixture. Let the veal chop rest for at least 10 minutes. Enjoy!

Italian Sausage Sliders

Servings: 16
Cooking Time: 6 Minutes

Ingredients:
- 2 pounds Johnsonville All Natural Ground Italian Sausage or Links (remove from casing)
- 1 pound ground beef
- 16 small slider buns or mini sandwich rolls
- Condiments
- Provolone cheese and Marinara sauce
- Fresh mozzarella, fresh basil, and sliced tomatoes
- Giardiniera – marinated chopped vegetables and olives
- Sauteed onions and roasted red peppers
- Sauteed mushrooms and Cheddar cheese

Directions:
1. Preheat the grill to 400°F using direct heat with a cast iron grate installed.
2. In a large bowl, combine sausage and beef. Using your hands, blend the two meats together and form into one large ball. Use a spoon or a small measuring cup to gather up about a 3 ounce ball and press into patties … with the Mini Burger Basket you can form and cook 12 Mini Burgers at once!
3. Place the Mini Burger Basket or individual sliders directly on the cooking grid. Cook for about 3 minutes then flip and continue cooking for another 3 minutes. The internal temperature should be 160°F.
4. Slice the buns and top the sliders with your favorite condiments.

Butter-rubbed Lamb Chops With Fig Mustard Aioli

Servings: 4

Cooking Time: 6 Minutes

Ingredients:
- 4 lamb chops
- 4 oz (225 g) butter, room temperature
- 2 tsp (10 ml) Classic Steakhouse Seasoning
- 1 tbsp (15ml) fig preserves
- Pinch of Ginger
- 1/2 tbsp (8 ml) soy sauce
- 3 tbsp (45 ml) German mustard
- 3 tbsp (45 ml) mayonnaise
- 1 tsp (5 g) tumeric
- 2 tbsp (30 ml) fig preserves
- Pinch of cayenne pepper

Directions:
1. Preheat the grill to 450°F using direct heat with a cast iron grate installed.
2. In a small bowl, mix all of the ingredients together except for the lamb. With the back of a spoon, smear half of the butter mixture onto the lamb chops. Place the lamb chops with the butter side up on the grid for 2-3 minutes (depending on the thickness you may choose to have them on each side longer.) Flip the chops and then smear the rest of the butter onto the chops. Grill for another 2-3 minutes or until desired temperature is reached, about 135°F for medium rare. Serve with Fig Mustard Aioli.
3. Combine all of the ingredients and mix very well; serve with the lamb chops.

Stir-fry Szechuan Beef

Servings: 4
Cooking Time: 7 Minutes

Ingredients:

- 1 pound Certified Angus Beef flank steak, cut against grain into ¼-inch thick strips
- 4 tbsp soy sauce, divided
- 4 tbsp rice wine (Shaoxing), divided
- 1 tbsp cornstarch
- 1 tbsp rice wine vinegar
- 2 tbsp canola oil
- 3 cloves garlic, minced
- 2 teaspoons Szechuan peppercorns, crushed (or 1-teaspoon of each, chili flake and black pepper)
- 2 tablespoons oyster sauce (or hoisin sauce)
- 10 small red chilies, halved and seeded
- 4 scallions, cut into 2-inch segments

Directions:

1. Combine 2 tablespoons soy sauce, 2 tablespoons rice wine, cornstarch and rice wine vinegar in a mixing bowl; whisk together. Add sliced flank steak and marinate for 30 minutes to 1 hour.
2. Preheat the grill to 500°F using direct heat with a cast iron grate installed.
3. Remove steak strips from marinade, pat dry and discard marinade. Heat the oil in a Carbon Steel Wok; add beef strips and stir constantly for 2-3 minutes to cook evenly.
4. Stir in garlic and Szechuan peppercorns and stir-fry another minute. Reduce heat to medium, add remaining soy sauce, rice wine, oyster sauce, chilies and scallions.
5. Sear 3-4 minutes, stirring often until sauce thickens and glazes meat. Enjoy!

Rack Of Lamb

Servings: 8
Cooking Time: 15 Minutes

Ingredients:

- 8 rib lamb rack, frenched
- Classic Steakhouse Seasoning
- Olive oil

Directions:

1. Remove the silver skin and trim excess fat from the lamb rack (you can leave the fat cap on or remove it – this is personal preference. If you leave it on, score the fat with a sharp knife). Cover the bones with foil. Smear the lamb with olive oil and generously rub with seasoning.
2. Preheat the grill to 225°F using direct heat with a cast iron grate installed.
3. Add a disposable drip pan to the platesetter to catch any drippings. Add the lamb and cook until the internal temperature hits 140°F. Remove from the kamado grill and rest under tented foil for 15 minutes.
4. While the lamb rests, carefully remove the platesetter to set the kamado grill for direct cooking. Open the vents to increase the kamado grill temperature to 550°F. Sear the outside of the lamb; re-season if necessary.
5. To serve, cut the lamb between the ribs.

Smoked Brisket Roll

Servings: 10
Cooking Time: 650 Minutes

Ingredients:
- 1 brisket flat, fat cap on, about 6 lbs (2.7 kg)
- 1 cup brisket rub
- ½ bag Jack Daniels wood chips, soaked overnight in water
- Bardough House Slaw
- 10 country loaf rolls
- Salted farm butter for the rolls
- 1½ cups (360 ml) brown sugar
- 1 cup (240 ml) kosher salt
- 1 cup (240 ml) ground espresso beans
- ¼ cup (60 ml) freshly ground black pepper
- ¼ cup (60 ml) garlic powder
- 2 Tbsp (30 ml) ground cinnamon
- 2 Tbsp (30 ml) ground cumin
- 2 Tbsp (30 ml) cayenne pepper
- 1½ cups (150 g) green cabbage, thinly sliced
- 1½ cups (150 g) red cabbage, thinly sliced
- 1¼ cups (150 g) julienned carrots
- 1/3 cup (40 g) dried cranberries
- 2 Tbsp (30 ml) mustard
- 1 cup (240 ml) mayo
- Salt to taste
- 1 lb (455 g) stone ground flour
- 1½ cups (355 g) filtered water
- 2¼ tsp (7 g) fresh yeast
- 5 g salt
- 3 Tbsp + 1 tsp (50 ml) extra virgin olive oil

Directions:
1. Coat the brisket on all sides with an even layer of rub. Let the meat to rest for 1 hour at room temperature or until the rub starts to turn pasty.
2. Preheat the grill to 225°F using direct heat with a cast iron grate installed.
3. Place the brisket, fat side up, on the grill. After 8 hours check meat periodically. Poke the meat in a few places; the fat should separate under your finger. When the brisket reaches an internal temperature of 200°F, remove it from the kamado grill onto a rimmed baking sheet to rest for 30 minutes.
4. Cut the brisket in thin slices against the grain. Cut the rolls in half and butter on both sides. Add sliced brisket and slaw and enjoy!
5. Mix all rub ingredients together and refrigerate.
6. Mix all slaw ingredients together and refrigerate.
7. Dissolve the yeast in half the water. Place the flour and salt in a mixing bowl; add the yeast mixture and the oil.
8. Knead the dough by hand for 10 minutes, slowly adding the rest of the water. Allow to rest for 1 hour or until double in size. Divide into 10 equal size rounds. Shape into balls and allow to rest for an additional hour.
9. Set the kamado grill for indirect cooking with the platesetter and a Pizza and Baking Stone at 400°F. Place the rolls 1 inch (2.5 cm) apart on the preheated stone. Spritz lightly with water and bake for 15 minutes, then remove to a cooling rack.

Dad's Grilled Steak

Servings: 4

Cooking Time: 15 Minutes

Ingredients:
- 1 sirloin steak (approximately 4 lb/1.8 kg and 3 inches/8 cm thick)
- 1/4 cup (60 ml) freshly ground black pepper
- 12 cloves garlic, minced
- 1 cup (250 ml) dry red wine
- 1/4 cup (60 ml) vegetable oil
- 1/4 cup (60 ml) ketchup
- 2 tbsp (30 ml) chopped fresh herbs (such as parsley, sage, rosemary)
- 1 tbsp (15 ml) Worcestershire sauce
- Salt to taste

Directions:
1. Rub the steak with the black pepper, pressing the seasoning into the meat.
2. In a glass dish large enough to hold the steak, whisk together the garlic, wine, vegetable oil, ketchup, herbs, Worcestershire sauce and salt. Add steak, turning once to coat. Marinate, covered and refrigerated, for 6 hours or overnight.
3. Preheat the grill to 450°F using direct heat with a cast iron grate installed.
4. Remove steak from marinade, discarding marinade. Pat dry with paper towels. Season steak with salt.
5. Grill steak for 12–15 minutes per side for medium-rare to medium doneness, drizzling with a little red wine occasionally to add some sizzling moisture. Remove from the kamado grill and let rest for 5–10 minutes. Thinly slice the steak across the grain and serve.

Grilled Entrecôte Of Beef

Servings: 4
Cooking Time: 20 Minutes

Ingredients:
- Guacamole
- Spice Rub and Entrecote
- Cheesy Tortillas
- 2 Ripe Avocados
- 1 Red Onion, Finely Chopped
- 2 Tomatoes, Inside Removed, then Cubed
- 1/2 Cup (120 ml) Cilantro, Roughly Chopped
- 1 Lemon, Zest and Juice
- 4 Ribeye Steaks
- 2 tbsp (30g) Coarse Salt
- 1 1/2 tbsp (20g) Surgar
- 2 tbsp (15g) Coriander Powder
- 2 tbsp (15g) Paprika
- 2 tbsp (5g) Garlic Flakes
- 1/2 tbsp (5g) Peppercorns
- 2 tbsp (5g) Onion Powder
- 2 tbsp (5g) Fresh Thyme
- 4 Tortillas
- 1/2 Cup (60g) Cheddar Cheese, Grated
- 1/3 Cup (80 ml) Parsley, Roughly Chopped
- Cayenne Pepper
- Lemon Zest

Directions:
1. Preheat the grill to 750°F using direct heat with a cast iron grate installed. Place the steaks on the grill and cook to the desired temperature. While the meat is resting before carving, lower the temperature to 400°F and place the tortillas on the grill, allowing the cheese to melt and the tortillas to get a crust. Cut the tortillas into quarters and serve with the guacamole.
2. Mesh the avocado to desired texture with a fork. Add the rest of the ingredients and mix well. Season to taste.
3. Place all rub ingredients in a mortar and pestle or spice grinder, and grind to just before it becomes fine. Rub generously over the steaks and refrigerate for an hour.
4. Mix all the ingredients and spread evenly over tortillas. Cover with the remaining tortillas and lightly press down. Be careful before braaing as the cheese may fall out.

Steak Roll-ups With Porcini Mushroom Rub

Servings: 4
Cooking Time: 70 Minutes

Ingredients:
- Coffee grinder or spice mill
- 2 heads garlic
- Olive oil
- Kosher salt and freshly ground black pepper to taste
- 2 portobello mushroom caps, soaked in warm water for 10 minutes
- 1 medium red onion, sliced into 1/2-inch (1 cm) thick rings
- 1/2 cup (125 mL) dried porcini mushroom caps
- 4 beef tenderloin steaks (approx. 8 oz/225 g each), cut 2 inches (5 cm) thick 1/4 cup (60 mL) fresh rosemary, chopped
- 4 strips bacon
- 4 1/2 tsp (22 mL) butter

Directions:
1. Preheat the grill to 500°F using direct heat with a cast iron grate installed.
2. Cut the tops off the garlic heads, exposing the cloves on the inside. Drizzle with olive oil and season with kosher salt and black pepper. Wrap them in a little bit of aluminum foil and roast for 30–45 minutes, until the cloves are tender. Remove from kamado grill and allow to cool for a few minutes. Squeeze the hot roasted garlic cloves from the heads. Set aside.
3. At the same time as you are roasting the garlic, grill the Portobello mushrooms and red onions for 10–15 minutes, until lightly charred and tender. Remove from kamado grill and allow to cool. Pat the mushrooms with paper towels to remove excess moisture. Thinly slice and set aside.
4. In a coffee grinder or spice mill, grind the porcini mushroom caps into a coarse powder.
5. Take a steak and stand it up on its side. Starting at the bottom of the steak, make an incision across the steak about 1/4 to 1/2 inch (0.5 to 1 cm) thick and 6 to 8 inches (15 to 20 cm) long. Next slice the steak across and roll it at the same time to cut the beef tenderloin into a long strip of meat about 1/2 inch (1 cm) thick. Repeat with remaining steaks.
6. Mash the roasted cloves of garlic, mix with a little drizzle of olive oil and season with salt and pepper. Set aside. Lay a strip of steak onto a flat work surface. Season both sides lightly with a little salt and black pepper and a liberal amount of porcini mushroom powder. Spread a little of the roasted garlic mixture across the entire surface of the steak. Sprinkle with some chopped rosemary leaves. Lay a few slices of grilled portobello mushroom and red onion
7. across the entire surface of the steak. Starting at one end, roll up the steak into a tight pinwheel. Take a strip of bacon and twist it up so it looks a little like a piece of bacon rope. Wrap the bacon around the steak roll-up, knot it and secure with a toothpick. Repeat.
8. Again, set the kamado grill for direct cooking at 500°F/260°C.
9. Grill roll-ups for 3–5 minutes per side, until the bacon is crisp and the meat is medium-rare. This is tenderloin, so it won't take too long. Just when the steaks are about done, place a little knob of butter on top of each steak, close lid and let it melt. Remove from grill, remove toothpicks and serve immediately.

Steak With Caramelized Onions

Servings: 2
Cooking Time: 5 Minutes

Ingredients:
- 1 shoulder steak
- 2 Tablespoons olive oil, separated
- 1 medium white onion, sliced
- 1 cup Miller LITE beer
- 1 tablespoon Plugra unsalted butter
- Salt and pepper, to taste

Directions:

1. Preheat the grill to 450°F using direct heat with a cast iron grate installed. In the meantime, heat a large skillet over medium high heat and add to tablespoons of the oil and swirl to coat well. Add the sliced onions. Sauté the onions until caramelized (about 4 minutes). Add beer and simmer until liquid is reduced by 75%. Add the butter and swirl until melted. Set aside and keep warm.

2. Rub all sides of the steak with one tablespoon of oil and season to taste with the salt and pepper. Place on hot grill and sear for three minutes per side. Lower the heat and continue to cook; turning often until done to your liking. Remove the steaks from the grill and let them rest for 5-8 minutes.

3. Place the steak on serving plates and spoon caramelized onions over the top.

Bacon Cheeseburger Hotdogs

Servings: 8

Cooking Time: 16 Minutes

Ingredients:

- 8 good-quality all-beef hot dogs
- 8 Cobblestone Bread Co.™ Spud Dogs
- drizzle of ketchup
- drizzle of mustard
- chopped fresh parsley
- cheeseburger mixture
- white cheddar cheese sauce
- 6 strips of bacon, diced
- 1 pound ground beef
- 1-14 ounce can diced tomatoes, drained
- 2 tablespoons ketchup
- 1 tablespoon yellow mustard
- 1 ½ cups grated sharp cheddar cheese, divided
- salt and black pepper
- 2 tablespoons unsalted butter
- 2 tablespoons all-purpose flour
- 1 ½ cups whole milk
- 1 ½ cup grated white cheddar cheese
- pinch of cayenne pepper
- salt and black pepper

Directions:

1. Preheat the grill to 425°F using direct heat with a cast iron grate installed, and add your hot dogs to the grill. Grill for about 2 minutes on each side or until charred and warm. Remove from heat.

2. Assemble your bacon cheeseburger hot dogs, by placing each hot dog on Cobblestone Bread Co.™ Spud Dog. Top with the cheeseburger mixture and spoon the cheese sauce on top. Drizzle with ketchup and yellow mustard. Sprinkle with fresh parsley and the reserved bacon. Enjoy!

3. In a large, nonstick skillet, add the bacon. Fry over medium-low heat until crispy. Transfer the bacon to a plate that has been lined with a paper towel and pour out most of the bacon grease from the skillet. Place it back on the stove, and increase the heat to medium. Add the beef to the pan and cook until brown and cooked through, about 8 minutes. Decrease the heat to low, and add most of the bacon (reserving about 2 tablespoons for garnish) diced tomatoes, ketchup, yellow mustard, cheddar cheese, and salt and black pepper. Stir until the cheese has melted. Cover and keep warm.

4. In a small saucepan, melt the butter for the white cheddar cheese sauce over medium heat. Whisk in the flour and cook for about 1 minute or until golden. Continuing to whisk, add the milk. Cook for about 3-4 minutes or until just slightly thickened. Remove from heat and stir in the white cheddar cheese until melted. Season with a pinch of cayenne pepper and salt and black pepper to taste. Cover and keep warm until you are ready to serve.

Dr. Bbq's Smoked Flat-cut Brisket With Coffee

Servings: 2

Cooking Time: 60 Minutes

Ingredients:
- 1 USDA Choice flat-cut brisket (5 to 6 pounds), fat left on
- Barbecue Rub #67
- ½ cup strong brewed coffee
- ½ cup Sugar in the Raw
- ½ cup kosher salt
- 3 tablespoons chili powder
- 3 tablespoons paprika
- 1 teaspoon garlic powder
- 1 teaspoon onion powder
- ½ teaspoon black pepper
- ½ teaspoon lemon pepper
- ½ teaspoon ground coffee
- ¼ teaspoon cayenne pepper

Directions:
1. Preheat the grill to 235°F using direct heat with a cast iron grate installed.
2. Season the brisket liberally with the rub. Cook the brisket fat-side down for 1 hour and then flip it to fat-side up. Cook to an internal temperature of 160°F.
3. Lay out a big double-thick layer of heavy-duty aluminum foil and lay the brisket on it fat-side up. Pull up the sides of the foil and pour on the coffee as you close up the package. Be careful not to puncture it or you'll have to start over. Return the brisket to the cooker. After another hour, begin checking the internal temperature. When it reaches 200°F, remove the brisket and let it rest for 30 minutes, wrapped. Remove the brisket from the foil. It desired, skim the fat from the liquid and serve the remaining juices as a sauce. Slice the brisket about ¼ inch thick to serve.
4. Combine all the ingredients in a medium bowl and mix well. The rub may be stored in an airtight container in a cool place for up to 6 months.

Smoked Beef Ribs With Mustard Marinade

Servings: 6

Cooking Time: 300 Minutes

Ingredients:
- 1 Certified Angus Beef block cut beef short ribs (3-bone in roast), approximately 5-8 lbs.
- 1 part Worcestershire sauce
- 1 part apple cider vinegar
- 2 parts yellow mustard
- 1 part whole grain mustard
- 1 part water
- 5 parts kosher salt
- 2 parts black pepper
- 2 parts garlic powder
- 1 part lemon pepper
- 1 part ancho chile powder
- Light touch of cayenne
- 1 cup honey
- 1 cup brown sugar
- ½ cup bouillon paste
- 1 cup beer, brown ale

Directions:

1. Preheat the grill to 250°F using direct heat with a cast iron grate installed. Brush the beef with the mustard marinade and season both sides of the beef liberally. Place the seasoned meat in the kamado grill and smoke for five hours. Remove the meat from the grill.
2. Mix all ingredients together.
3. Mix all ingredients together.
4. Slather the smoked ribs with the glaze and wrap with foil. Put the wrapped ribs back in the kamado grill and cook for one more hour.

Rouladen

Servings: 6
Cooking Time: 45 Minutes

Ingredients:
- 1 (1 1/2-2lb) flank steak
- 1/2 cup chopped onion
- 1/3 cup chopped dill pickle
- 1/4 cup German mustard
- 1/2 tsp salt
- 1/4 tsp pepper
- 6 strips of bacon, separated

Directions:
1. In a medium skillet, brown 3 strips of bacon until crisp. Remove from the pan.
2. Remove all by 2 Tablespoon of the bacon fat and cook the onion over medium heat or until the onion is translucent. Set aside to cool.
3. Pound flank steak into an 8 inch by 10 inch rectangle.
4. Spread the meat with the mustard.
5. Top the meat with the onion, dill pickle, and crumbled cooked bacon.
6. Roll the meat around the filling lengthwise.
7. Wrap the roast with the remaining raw bacon and secure with metal skewers.
8. Grilling:
9. Preheat the grill to 425°F using direct heat with a cast iron grate installed. Place the roast on the grid and cook for 30-45 minutes or until the internal temperature reaches 130°F.
10. Allow the rouladen to rest for 20 minutes before carving.

Holiday Sirloin Roast

Servings: 6
Cooking Time:180 Minutes

Ingredients:
- 1 (5-8 lb) sirloin roast
- 1/4 cup Dijon mustard
- 2 Tablespoons fresh rosemary, chopped
- 1/2 tsp salt
- 1/4 tsp pepper
- 3 cloves garlic, minced

Directions:
1. Bring the roast to room temperature for 30 minutes before cooking.
2. Sprinkle the roast with salt and pepper.
3. Spread liberally with Dijon and press rosemary and garlic into the mustard.
4. Grilling:
5. Preheat the grill to 325°F using direct heat with a cast iron grate installed.
6. Place the roast directly on the grid and close the dome for 2 1/2 to 3 hours or until the internal temperature reaches 130°F.
7. Remove from the grill onto a board and allow it to rest for 20 minutes before carving.

Beef Asparagus Stir Fry

Servings:4
Cooking Time: 10 Minutes

Ingredients:

- 1 lb. boneless beef short rib, sliced thin
- ½ cup soy sauce
- ¼ cup oyster sauce
- 2 tsp corn starch
- 1 tbsp rice wine vinegar
- 3 cloves garlic, minced
- 2 tbsp ginger, minced
- 2 tbsp canola oil
- 1 bunch of asparagus, cut in to 1" segments
- Chopped green onion for garnish

Directions:

1. One day before the cook mix together the soy sauce, oyster sauce, corn starch, rice wine vinegar, garlic and ginger. Marinate the beef overnight in the mixture.
2. Preheat the grill to 500°F using direct heat with a cast iron grate installed(close the bottom vent before adding the wok).
3. Heat the canola oil in the wok. Add the marinated beef and stir fry. Once the sauce reduces and becomes a nice glaze, add the asparagus and stir fry until bright green.
4. Serve over rice and garnish with chopped green onion.

Chris Lane's Rib-eye Steaks On The Egg

Servings:4
Cooking Time: 16 Minutes

Ingredients:

- 4 (1 inch thick) rib-eye steaks
- ¼ cup olive oil
- Tony Chachere's Seasoning
- 1 pound asparagus
- 1-2 tbsp olive oil
- Tony Chachere's Seasoning

Directions:

1. Preheat the grill to 550°F using direct heat with a cast iron grate installed.
2. Using a basting brush, lightly coat each of the rib-eye steaks with the olive oil, season with Tony Chachere's Seasoning, and set aside.
3. Place the steaks on the grid and close the lid. Cook for 3 minutes. Turn the steaks over and continue cooking for 3 more minutes for medium-rare.
4. Transfer the steaks to a platter and let the steaks rest for 5 minutes. Slice across the grain and serve with a baked potato and grilled asparagus.
5. Prepare the asparagus by breaking or cutting off any tough bottom. Coat the asparagus with olive oil and sprinkle with Tony Chachere's Seasoning.
6. Grill the asparagus spears for 5-10 minutes, until nicely charred and fork tender, turning them every few minutes so that they brown relatively evenly.

Italian Meatballs

Servings: 12
Cooking Time: 30 Minutes

Ingredients:

- 1/4 cup panko breadcrumbs, lightly toasted
- 3/4lb (340g) Roma tomatoes, peeled and chopped
- 2 tbsp extra virgin olive oil, divided
- 1/2 tbsp nonpareil capers, drained and chopped
- 1/2 tsp dried oregano
- 1/2 tsp dried marjoram
- 1 tbsp fresh basil, plus more for serving, chopped
- 1/3lb (150g) ground pork
- 1/3lb (150g) ground beef
- 1/3lb (150g) ground veal
- 3 tsp whole milk
- 1 large egg, lightly beaten
- 2 pitted Kalamata olives, minced
- 1 tbsp grated Parmesan cheese, plus more for serving
- 1 tbsp fresh flat-leaf parsley, minced
- 1 tsp kosher salt, plus more as needed
- freshly ground black pepper

Directions:

1. Preheat the grill to 375°F (191°C) using indirect heat with a standard grate and a cast iron skillet installed.
2. On a rimmed sheet pan, place breadcrumbs in a single layer and toast until beginning to brown, about 3 to 5 minutes. Remove the pan from the grill and set aside.
3. Place tomatoes in a food processor and purée. Place tomatoes and 1 tbsp oil in the skillet. Bring to a boil, slightly close the top and bottom vents to reduce the temperature to 325°F (163°C), close the lid, and simmer until the sauce starts to thicken, about 5 minutes, stirring occasionally.
4. Add capers, oregano, and marjoram to the skillet, and simmer until the sauce has reduced to 1 1/4 cups, about 5 minutes. Add basil, season with salt to taste, and set aside.
5. In a large bowl, combine pork, beef, and veal. Add breadcrumbs, milk, egg, olives, Parmesan cheese, parsley, and salt, and mix well with your hands. Shape the mixture into 12 meatballs.
6. Slightly open the top and bottom vents to return the temperature to 375°F (191°C). Once the grill reaches the needed temperature, return the skillet to the grill and heat the remaining 1 tbsp oil until shimmering. Place the meatballs in the skillet, close the lid, and cook until they start to brown, about 8 minutes, turning once every 2 minutes. Add the sauce, close the lid, and cook until the meatballs are cooked through and the sauce is hot, about 8 minutes.
7. Remove the meatballs from the grill, place on a large serving platter, and top with more Parmesan cheese and basil. Serve immediately.

Smoked & Braised Beef Chuck Steak

Servings: 8
Cooking Time: 210 Minutes

Ingredients:

- 2 1/2 lb (1.2 kg) thick-cut chuck steak
- 1 large yellow onion, halved
- 1 green bell pepper, halved
- 4 tbsp extra virgin olive oil
- 4 garlic cloves, smashed
- 4 carrots, cut into 1/2-in (1.25-cm) pieces
- 3 celery stalks, cut into 1-in (2.5-cm) pieces
- peels of 2 oranges, thinly sliced
- 1/2 cup fruity red wine
- 2 1/2 cups beef or chicken stock
- kosher salt and freshly ground black pepper
- for the rub
- 1/4 cup kosher salt
- 4 tbsp ground black pepper
- 2 tbsp garlic salt
- 1 tbsp paprika
- 1 tbsp ground cayenne pepper
- 1/4 cup raw sugar
- to smoke
- post oak, wine barrel, or grapevine wood chunks

Directions:

1. To make the rub, in a small bowl, combine all the rub ingredients. Rub spice mixture all over steak to ensure even and full coverage. Wrap tightly with plastic wrap and refrigerate for 4 to 24 hours. Before smoking, remove steak from the fridge and allow to come to room temperature.

2. Preheat the grill to 350°F (177°C). Once hot, add the wood chunks and install the heat deflector and a drip pan. Install a cast iron grate with a dutch oven on the grate. Place onion and pepper on the grate, close the lid, and grill until beginning to soften and char, about 7 to 10 minutes. Transfer onion and pepper to a cutting board and thinly slice. Set aside.

3. Place steak on the grate, close the lid, and smoke until the internal temperature reaches 190°F (88°C), about 45 minutes. Remove steak from the grill and let rest for 10 to 15 minutes. (Cut into large pieces for braising if needed.)

4. To braise the meat, heat oil in the dutch oven until shimmering. Add the smoked steak and the grilled onion and pepper to the dutch oven along with garlic, carrots, celery, orange peels, wine, and stock. (Steak should be fully submerged in liquid). Leaving the dutch oven uncovered, close the grill lid and cook until steak is tender, about 2 1/2 hours, turning once halfway through.

5. Transfer steak to a cutting board, thickly slice across the grain, and arrange on a large serving platter along with some of the braised vegetables. Skim any fat from the braising liquid and spoon some of the liquid over the steak and vegetables. Season with salt and pepper to taste. Serve immediately.

Smoked Goat Bolognese

Servings: 8
Cooking Time: 150 Minutes

Ingredients:
- 1 1/2 lb (680g) boneless goat leg
- kosher salt and freshly ground black pepper
- 1–2 tsp sweet smoked paprika
- 1 medium yellow onion, chopped
- 4 garlic cloves, chopped
- 3 celery stalks, diced
- 2 carrots, diced
- 1 1/2 cups beer
- 1 1/2 cups cola
- 1 lb (450g) dried rigatoni
- olive oil
- for the sauce
- 1 tbsp olive oil
- 1 white onion, diced
- 4 garlic cloves, minced
- 15oz (425g) can crushed tomatoes
- 1 cup red wine
- 1 tsp fresh oregano, minced
- 1/2 cup heavy cream
- to smoke
- cherry or wine barrel wood chunks

Directions:

1. About 2 to 3 hours before cooking, coat goat leg liberally with salt, pepper, and a light (but thorough) dusting of paprika. Cover with plastic wrap and allow to come to room temperature.

2. Preheat the grill to 250°F (121°C). Once hot, add the wood chunks, then install the heat deflector and a standard grate with a dutch oven on the grate. Add onion, garlic, celery, and carrots to the dutch oven. Close the grill lid and sweat the vegetables for 5 minutes. Stir in beer and cola, and add goat leg.

3. Loosely cover the dutch oven with aluminum foil, close the grill lid, and smoke until the internal temperature reaches 190°F (88°C), about 1 to 2 hours, checking the temperature every hour. Transfer goat leg to a large serving platter and let rest for 30 to 45 minutes, then shred the meat. Season with salt and pepper to taste. Set aside.

4. Cook the rigatoni on the stovetop according to package directions. Drain and rinse with cold water, and toss with a little olive oil to prevent sticking. Set aside.

5. To make the sauce, on the stovetop in a large skillet over medium heat, heat oil until shimmering. Add onions and garlic, and sauté until fragrant and beginning to brown, about 2 to 3 minutes. Add tomatoes, wine, and oregano. Cook until reduced by one-fourth, about 10 to 15 minutes.

6. Add shredded meat, cream, and cooked rigatoni to the skillet. Stir gently and cook until thick, about 5 to 7 minutes. Season with salt and pepper to taste, and serve warm.

Grilled Cheesesteak Pizza

Servings: 4

Cooking Time: 8 Minutes

Ingredients:
- 1 tablespoon extra-virgin olive oil
- 1 roasted red bell pepper, sliced
- 1/2 onion, sliced
- 1 (14.5 ounce) can Red Gold Diced Tomatoes, drained
- 1/2 tablespoon dried oregano
- 5 ounces Laura's Lean Beef Sirloin Steak, cooked and thinly sliced
- 1-10 to 11 ounce container pizza dough, your favorite recipe or store bought
- 2 tablespoons Red Gold Tomato Paste
- 2 ounces shredded provolone cheese
- 2 ounces shredded low-fat cheddar cheese
- 1 tablespoon chopped fresh parsley

Directions:
1. Preheat the grill to 600°F using direct heat with a cast iron grate installed.
2. Heat olive oil in a Cast Iron Skillet. Add the red bell pepper, onions and tomatoes (reserve ¼ cup of the tomatoes) and cook together until onions are soft. Remove from the skillet, sprinkle with oregano and set aside.
3. In the skillet, grill steaks to desired temperature. Remove the skillet from the grill, slice the steak into thin pieces.
4. Add the platesetter for indirect cooking and reduce the heat to 450°F. Preheat a Pizza & Baking Stone.
5. Divide pizza dough in half and roll each half out into a circle on a Dough Rolling Mat, getting it as thin as possible.
6. Gently lay one of the crusts onto the Stone. Cook about 1 to 2 minutes per side, depending on temperature of grill. Use tongs to flip and cook each side of the crust. If bubbles appear, just prick the dough bubble and keep cooking. Repeat for the second crust.
7. Spread 1 tablespoon of tomato paste on each crust. Divide and top each pizza with the tomato mixture, beef and cheese. Carefully return one pizza to the Stone. Cook an additional 3 to 4 minutes until cheese is melted. Repeat for the second pizza (keep a close watch on pizzas, removing if the crust is getting toasty).
8. Sprinkle with the ¼ cup tomatoes that were set aside along with the fresh parsley. Serve immediately.

Antelope Medallions

Servings: 4
Cooking Time: 15 Minutes

Ingredients:
- 2 antelope tenderloins, 2lb (1kg) in total, cut into 8 medallions
- 4 tbsp olive oil
- for the marinade
- 3 1/2 tsp extra virgin olive oil
- 1/2 tsp sesame oil
- 2 tbsp brandy
- 1 garlic clove, minced
- 1/8 tsp kosher salt
- 1/8 tsp ground black pepper
- for the sauce
- 1 tbsp olive oil
- 1 shallot, minced
- 1 garlic clove, minced
- 1/4 cup brandy
- 1 cup beef stock
- 2 tbsp heavy cream
- 1 tsp hot sauce
- kosher salt and freshly ground black pepper

Directions:
1. To make the marinade, in a large bowl, whisk together olive oil, sesame oil, brandy, garlic, salt, and pepper. Place antelope in the marinade, cover with plastic wrap, and refrigerate for 2 hours.
2. Preheat the grill to 400°F (204°C) using direct heat with a cast iron grate installed and a cast iron skillet on the grate. Remove the medallions from the marinade, pat dry with paper towels, and coat with olive oil on all sides. Place the medallions on the grate (not in the skillet), close the lid, and grill until the internal temperature reaches 160°F (71°C), about 3 to 5 minutes per side, flipping once.
3. To make the sauce, in the hot skillet, heat oil until shimmering. Add shallot and garlic, and sauté until they begin to brown, about 2 minutes. Add brandy and flambé. (The heat of the pan should create a burst of flame.) When the flames subside, add stock, cream, and hot sauce. Close the lid and cook until the sauce has reduced to 1/4 cup, about 5 to 8 minutes.
4. Remove the medallions from the grill, spoon sauce over top, and serve immediately.

Smoked Oxtail Stew

Servings: 6
Cooking Time: 240 Minutes

Ingredients:

- 3.5 lbs Oxtails
- 4 stalks celery, medium chopped
- 2 onions, medium chopped
- 8 oz cremini mushrooms, halved
- 1 small butternut squash, medium chopped
- 4 carrots, medium chopped
- Olive oil, salt, pepper (to brown)
- 6 tsp all purpose flour
- 3 tsp Louisiana Hot Sauce
- 1 tbs Creole seasoning
- 1 tbs granulated garlic
- 1 tbs fresh garlic
- 3 tbs whole grain dijon mustard
- 4 cups beef stock
- 2 tbs soy sauce
- 3 tbs ketchup
- 3 sprigs rosemary
- 2 x 14 oz cans chopped tomatoes
- 2 tbs salt
- 2 tbs pepper
- Mesquite and cherry wood, soaked in water
- Deep roaster foil pain (about 12" x 10" x 4")

Directions:

1. Oil, salt, and pepper the oxtails; brown on the grill with the cooking grid only. Let oxtails rest after browning.
2. Preheat the grill to 350°F using direct heat with a cast iron grate installed.
3. Cut all vegetables. Mix stock, mustard, soy, ketchup, and tomatoes in separate bowl. Place all vegetables, herbs, tails, and flour in a bowl and toss. Place mixture in a deep roasting pan and add liquid. Place soaked wood on fire and smoke for 4 hours at 350°F. Halfway through, cover with foil and stop adding wood.
4. After 4 hours, check tails for tenderness.
5. Enjoy with your favorite starch addition rice, potatoes, or pasta.

Wild Mushroom And Blue Cheese Stuffed Burger

Servings: 4

Cooking Time: 10 Minutes

Ingredients:
- 2 lbs (900 g) ground venison or sirloin
- Salt and pepper, for seasoning
- 2 1/2 tbsp (37 ml) hot sauce
- 10 oz (285 g) mixed wild mushrooms, sautéed and drained
- 8 oz (115 g) blue cheese, crumbled
- Arugula for garnish

Directions:

1. Mix the hot sauce into the ground meat, then divide the meat into eight equal portions, 1/4 pound (113 g) each. Take one of the divided ground meat and form it in a small cup.
2. Fill center with the mushrooms and 6 oz (90 g) blue cheese. Place remaining ground meat on top and seal.
3. Preheat the grill to 400°F using direct heat with a cast iron grate installed. Cook burgers for 3 to 5 minutes per side depending on desired doneness. Top with remaining blue cheese and arugula.

Jim Beam Hamburgers

Servings: 2

Cooking Time: 12 Minutes

Ingredients:
- 1 pound ground beef
- 1 (1 oz) package onion soup mix
- 2 tablespoons Worcestershire sauce
- 2 tablespoons Jim Beam bourbon
- Dash hot pepper sauce (recommended: Tabasco)
- Hamburger buns, for serving

Directions:

1. Preheat the grill to 375°F using direct heat with a cast iron grate installed. Using your hands, combine all ingredients in a medium bowl, mixing just to combine. Divide meat into 4 portions and form each into patty using your hands. Grill for 4 to 6 minutes on both sides for medium-rare to medium doneness. If desired, place buns, cut side down on the grill, until toasted, about 1 to 2 minutes. Serve burgers on buns.

BURGERS

Breakfast Burger

Servings: 4
Cooking Time: 13 Minutes

Ingredients:
- 1 1/2 lb ground beef
- 1/2 lb ground pork breakfast sausage
- 2 Tablespoon butter
- 8 strips bacon
- 4 slices sharp cheddar cheese
- 4 Brioche buns
- 4 eggs
- 4 thick slices tomato

Directions:
1. In a medium bowl, mix ground beef and sausage until just combined.
2. Form into 4 patties and refrigerate while the grill heats.
3. Melt butter in a large skillet and fry the eggs for 2 minutes on each side.
4. Grilling:
5. Preheat the grill to 400°F using direct heat with a cast iron grate installed.
6. Place bacon on a small cookie sheet and place on the grid in the grill. Cook until crispy.
7. Place the patties on the grid and close the dome for 3 minutes.
8. Flip the burgers and replace the dome for an additional 3 minutes.
9. Close all of the vents and allow the burgers to sit for an additional 5 minutes. The internal temperature of the burger should be 150°F.
10. Place cheese on top of the burgers and cover for 1 more minute.
11. Assemble the burgers by placing a burger on the bottom bun, topping with bacon, tomato, and a fried egg.

Classic American Burger

Servings: 4
Cooking Time: 12 Minutes

Ingredients:

- 2 lbs ground beef
- 1/2 tsp salt
- 1/4 tsp pepper
- 4 slices American cheese
- 4 hamburger buns
- Green Leaf Lettuce
- Sliced Tomato
- Ketchup
- Mustard
- Sliced Pickle

Directions:

1. Form ground beef into four patties and season both sides with salt and pepper.
2. Grilling:
3. Preheat the grill to 500°F using direct heat with a cast iron grate installed.
4. Place burgers on the grid and close the dome for 3 minutes.
5. Flip burgers and close the dome for 2 more minutes.
6. Close all of the vents and allow the burgers to sit for 5 minutes.
7. Top each burger with a slice of cheese and close the dome for 1 more minute.
8. Build burgers with lettuce, tomato, pickle, mustard, and ketchup.

Oahu Burger

Servings: 4
Cooking Time: 12 Minutes

Ingredients:

- 2 lbs ground beef
- 1/4 cup thickened Teriyaki Marinade
- 1/4 cup mayonnaise
- 1/2 tsp sambal or sriracha
- 4 slices fresh pineapple, cored
- 4 slices tomato
- 4 slices butter lettuce
- 4 Hawaiian hamburger buns

Directions:

1. Form ground beef into four patties and season both sides with salt and pepper.
2. In a small bowl, mix mayonnaise with hot chile sauce and spread on buns.
3. Top each bun with a burger, slice of pineapple, lettuce and tomato.
4. Grilling:
5. Preheat the grill to 500°F using direct heat with a cast iron grate installed.
6. Place burgers on the grid and close the dome for 3 minutes.
7. Flip burgers, baste with Teriyaki Marinade, and place the pineapple slices on the grid. Close the dome for 2 more minutes.
8. Flip the burgers again and baste with remaining Teriyaki Marinade. Close the dome.
9. Close all of the vents and allow the burgers to sit for 5 minutes.

Quesadilla Burger

Servings: 4
Cooking Time: 12 Minutes

Ingredients:
- 2 lbs ground beef
- 2 Tablespoons Adobo Rub
- 1 cup shredded cheddar cheese
- 4 large flour tortillas
- Sour Cream
- Guacamole
- Salsa

Directions:
1. Form ground beef into four patties and season both sides with Adobo Rub.
2. Serve each burger with sour cream, guacamole, and salsa.
3. Grilling:
4. Preheat the grill to 500°F using direct heat with a cast iron grate installed.
5. Place burgers on the grid and close the dome for 3 minutes.
6. Flip burgers and close the dome for 2 more minutes.
7. Close all of the vents and allow the burgers to sit for 5 minutes.
8. Remove burgers and place flour tortillas on the grid.
9. Top each tortilla with shredded cheese and close the dome for 1 minute until the cheese melts.
10. Place a hamburger in the center of each tortilla and begin folding the tortilla around the burger like an envelope.

The Crowned Jewels Burger

Servings: 4
Cooking Time: 12 Minutes

Ingredients:
- 2 lbs ground beef
- 1/2 tsp salt
- 1/4 tsp pepper
- 1 lb thinly sliced pastrami
- 1 cup shredded Romaine lettuce
- 1/4 cup mayonnaise
- 2 Tablespoons ketchup
- 1/8 tsp onion powder
- 4 slices Sharp Cheddar cheese
- 4 hamburger buns
- 1 tomato, sliced

Directions:
1. Form ground beef into four patties and season both sides with salt and pepper.
2. Meanwhile, mix together mayonnaise, ketchup, and onion powder. Smear on each bun.
3. Place each pastrami and cheese covered burger on the prepared buns and top with shredded lettuce and tomato.
4. Grilling:
5. Preheat the grill to 500°F using direct heat with a cast iron grate installed.
6. Place burgers on the grid and close the dome for 3 minutes.
7. Flip burgers and close the dome for 2 more minutes.
8. Close all of the vents and allow the burgers to sit for 5 minutes.
9. Top each burger with 1/4 of the pastrami and a slice of cheese and close the dome for 1 more minute.

"the Masterpiece"

Servings: 4
Cooking Time: 12 Minutes

Ingredients:
- 2 lbs ground beef
- 6 ounces sliced mushrooms
- 4 Tablespoons shredded smoked Gouda
- 2 Tablespoons butter
- 2 Tablespoons olive oil
- 2 Tablespoons Dijon mustard
- 1/2 tsp salt
- 1/4 tsp pepper
- 8 slices bacon, cooked and crumbled
- 4 slices Swiss cheese
- 4 brioche buns
- 1 small onion, sliced

Directions:
1. Heat a skillet over medium heat and add 1 Tablespoon butter and 1 Tablespoon olive oil.
2. Place mushrooms in the pan and DO NOT MOVE THEM. Saute for 5-7 minutes or until the mushrooms are browned. Remove from the pan and set aside.
3. In the same skillet, heat remaining butter and olive oil and add onions. Saute over medium heat until they become translucent and begin to brown, about 10 minutes. Remove from the heat and set aside to cool.
4. Mix onion, mushrooms, and crumbled bacon.
5. Grilling:
6. Preheat the grill to 425°F using direct heat with a cast iron grate installed.
7. Form ground beef into eight patties and season both sides with salt and pepper.
8. Place a generous spoonful of the mushroom and onion mixture in the center of four patties and top with smoked Gouda.
9. Top with additional patty and press sides to seal the mixture inside.
10. Place burgers on the grid and close the dome for 5 minutes.
11. Flip burgers and close the dome for 3 more minutes.
12. Close all of the vents and allow the burgers to sit for 5 minutes.
13. Top each burger with a slice of Swiss cheese and close the dome for 1 more minute.
14. Spread buns with mustard, top with burgers and bun tops.

PORK

Bbq Chicken Quarters

Servings: 4
Cooking Time: 45

Ingredients:

- 4 skin-on, bone-in chicken leg quarters
- for the brine
- 1/2 cup kosher salt
- 1/2 cup packed light brown sugar
- 3 tbsp pickling spice
- 6 cups hot water
- for the sauce
- 1/4 cup molasses
- 2 cups ketchup
- 3 tsp Worcestershire sauce
- 2 tbsp lemon juice
- 1/2 tsp Tabasco sauce
- 3/8 cup packed dark brown sugar
- 1/2 tsp ground cayenne pepper
- 2 garlic cloves, finely minced
- 1 tbsp ground black pepper
- for the rub
- 4 tbsp kosher salt
- 4 tbsp ground black pepper
- 2 tbsp ancho powder

Directions:

1. To make the brine, in a medium bowl, whisk together salt, brown sugar, pickling spice, and water until salt and sugar have dissolved. Add ice cubes a few at a time until the liquid is no longer hot. Place chicken in a resealable plastic bag and add brine to cover. (Any extra brine can be refrigerated and saved for a later use.) Refrigerate for 1 hour.
2. To make the BBQ sauce, in a small saucepan, combine all the sauce ingredients. Place the saucepan on the stovetop over medium heat and simmer for 15 minutes, stirring occasionally. Remove from the heat and set aside.
3. To make the rub, in a small bowl, combine salt, pepper, and ancho powder. Remove chicken from the brine, pat dry with paper towels, and season with some of the rub mixture. Let chicken come to room temperature.
4. Preheat the grill to 425°F (218°C) using indirect heat with a cast iron grate installed. Brush chicken with the BBQ sauce and place on the grate. Close the lid and grill until the internal temperature reaches 170°F (77°C), 20 to 30 minutes, turning to evenly crisp the skin. Brush chicken with the BBQ sauce every 10 minutes while cooking.
5. Remove chicken from the grill and season with more rub mixture to taste. Let rest for 10 minutes. Serve with the remaining BBQ sauce.

Pork Belly Burnt Ends

Servings: 2
Cooking Time: 180 Minutes

Ingredients:
- 1 pound piece of pork belly
- Your favorite barbecue rub
- Your favorite barbecue sauce
- Honey
- Apple juice

Directions:
1. Preheat the grill to 275°F using direct heat with a cast iron grate installed.
2. Trim the pork belly and cut the pork belly into 1" cubes. Cover the pork belly pieces in your favorite BBQ rub. Place pork belly pieces on the cooking grid and smoke for 3 hours, spraying with apple juice every hour until the pork reaches and internal temperature of 190°F.
3. Remove the pork pieces from the kamado grill and place them in an aluminum pan. Toss the pork belly pieces with BBQ sauce until evenly covered. Drizzle with honey and put the aluminum pan back on the grill. Cook the pork belly and cook for another hour until the sauce has reduced and caramelized.

Pulled Pork Baked Beans

Servings: 6
Cooking Time: 60 Minutes

Ingredients:
- 3 cans Navy beans (drained and rinsed)
- 1 lb. pulled pork
- ¾ cup chicken stock
- 2 tsp kosher salt
- 3 tbsp Sweet & Smoky Kansas City Style BBQ Sauce
- 2 tbsp Vidalia Onion Sriracha BBQ Sauce

Directions:
1. Preheat the grill to 350°F using direct heat with a cast iron grate installed.
2. Into the dutch oven, add beans, pork, chicken stock, salt, and BBQ sauces. Let simmer for 45 min to an hour.
3. Let cool for 5-10 minutes, serve and enjoy!

Sunday Dinner Pork Roast

Servings: 6
Cooking Time: 60 Minutes

Ingredients:
- 1 (3-4 lb) boneless pork loin roast
- 1/4 cup olive oil, separated
- 2 Tablespoons fresh thyme, chopped
- 2 Tablespoons Worcestershire sauce
- 1 Tablespoon soy sauce
- 4 cloves garlic, minced
- 2 lb small potatoes, halved (we like Yukon golds)
- 1 lb carrots, cut into 2 inch chunks
- 1 onion, cut into 2 inch chunks

Directions:
1. In a small bowl, combine Worcestershire sauce, soy sauce, thyme, garlic, and 2 Tablespoon olive oil.
2. Rinse and pat the pork loin dry.
3. In the bottom of a roasting pan, toss onion, potatoes and carrots with 2 Tablespoon olive oil, salt, and pepper.
4. Place the pork loin on top of the vegetables, fat side up and brush with the Worcestershire sauce mixture.
5. Grilling:
6. Preheat the grill to 425°F using direct heat with a cast iron grate installed.
7. Place the roasting pan on the grid and close the dome for 45 minutes to 1 hour or until the roast reaches an internal temperature of 150°F.
8. Allow the roast to rest for 10 minutes before slicing and serve with roasted vegetables on the side.

Cherry-smoked Turkey Legs

Servings: 6
Cooking Time: 180 Minutes

Ingredients:
- 4 whole turkey legs, about 2.5lb (1.4kg) each
- kosher salt and freshly ground black pepper
- for the brine
- 1/2 cup kosher salt
- 1/2 cup packed light brown sugar
- 3 tbsp pickling spice
- 6 cups hot water
- for the glaze
- 12oz (340g) fresh or frozen cranberries
- 1 tbsp grated fresh ginger
- 1 tsp ground cloves
- 1 1/2 cups maple syrup
- 1 cup water
- to smoke
- cherry, peach, or apple wood chunks

Directions:
1. To make the brine, in a large bowl, whisk together salt, brown sugar, pickling spice, and water until salt and sugar have dissolved. Add ice cubes until the liquid is no longer hot. Place turkey legs in two large resealable plastic bags and add brine to cover. Refrigerate for 3 to 24 hours. Before grilling, remove turkey from the brine, pat dry with paper towels, and refrigerate uncovered for 2 hours. (Any extra brine can be refrigerated and saved for a later use.)
2. Preheat the grill to 275°F (135°C). Once hot, add the wood chunks and install the heat deflector and a standard grate. Remove turkey legs from the fridge and let come to room temperature.
3. To make the glaze, in a medium saucepan, combine cranberries, ginger, cloves, syrup, and water. Place the saucepan on the stovetop over medium heat and bring to a gentle boil. Cook until the cranberry skins burst and the mixture thickens, about 10 to 15 minutes. Don't overcook to the point where the syrup begins to smell like scorched sugar.
4. Place turkey legs on the grate, close the lid, and smoke for 1 hour. After 1 hour, brush with glaze every 15 minutes until the meat reaches an internal temperature of 180°F (82°C) degrees, about 1 to 2 more hours.
5. Remove turkey legs from the grill, let rest for 15 minutes, and slice. Serve with any remaining glaze.

Double Smoked Maple Bourbon Glazed Ham

Servings: 4

Cooking Time: 180 Minutes

Ingredients:
- 1 bone-in half spiral ham
- 3 cups apple juice
- 1 yellow onion, chopped
- 2 tbsp yellow mustard
- BBQ rub
- 1/2 cup pineapple juice
- 1/2 cup maple syrup
- 1 cup bourbon
- 1/4 tsp Dijon mustard
- 1 tsp cinnamon
- 1 cup brown sugar

Directions:
1. Preheat the grill to 275°F using direct heat with a cast iron grate installed.
2. Cover the ham in yellow mustard and add the BBQ rub. Put the apple juice and onion in a roasting pan then place the ham in a roasting rack in the roasting pan. Cook uncovered for 2 hours. Cover with foil and cook another hour. Uncover the ham, glaze, and cook for 30 minutes until the ham reaches an internal temperature of 140°.
3. Remove the ham from the kamado grill and let rest for 10 minutes. Slice and serve.
4. Add glaze ingredients to pan, bring to a boil, and reduce. Cook for 30 minutes or to your desired thickness.

Dill Pickle Injected Chicken Bog

Servings: 4
Cooking Time: 40 Minutes

Ingredients:
- 2 boneless, skinless chicken breasts
- Dill Pickle Hot sauce
- 4 cheddarwurst sausages
- 4 stalks celery, chopped
- ½ onion, minced
- 4 cloves of garlic, minced
- 1 qt. water
- 1 chicken bouillon cube
- 2 cups white rice
- Salt and pepper to taste

Directions:
1. Preheat the grill to 400°F using direct heat with a cast iron grate installed. Place the half-moon cast iron griddle with the flat side up on top of the grid and the dutch oven on the other half of the grid.
2. Season the chicken with salt and pepper, and inject with dill pickle hot sauce. Let the chicken marinate for 30 minutes.
3. Cook the chicken and sausages on the plancha until the chicken is cooked through and the sausages have some color, about 15-20 minutes.
4. While the chicken and sausages are cooking, add water, bouillon cube, garlic, onion, celery into the dutch oven. Remove the chicken and sausages, cube into bite size pieces, and add to the dutch oven. Add rice to the dutch oven and put the lid on. Cook for 20 minutes until rice is fully cooked, making sure to stir.
5. Remove from the grill, enjoy!

Chile Rubbed Grilled Pork Chops

Servings:8

Cooking Time: 8 Minutes

Ingredients:
- 4 boneless sirloin pork chops, about 6-oz each, 1/2 inch thick
- 2 cloves garlic, crushed
- 1 tablespoon ground cumin
- 1 teaspoon red pepper flakes
- 1/2 cup fresh lime juice
- 1/2 teaspoon salt
- 1/4 teaspoon black pepper, freshly ground
- 3 jalapeno Chile, seeded, very finely minced, about 1/4 cup
- 2 tablespoons sesame oil
- 2 tablespoons soy sauce
- 1/8 teaspoon sugar

Directions:

1. Stir together jalapeno, sesame oil, soy sauce and sugar together in a small bowl. Wearing disposable gloves, rub mixture over all surfaces of chops. Place chops in single layer in shallow dish. In a large measuring cup, stir together all marinade ingredients; pour over chops, set aside for 20-30 minutes.
2. Preheat the grill to 400°F using direct heat with a cast iron grate installed.
3. Remove chops from marinade, discarding marinade. Grill chops on grill, turning once, to medium doneness, about 3-4 minutes per side, until internal temperature on a thermometer reads 145°F, followed by a 3-minute rest time.
4. Best served with avocado-corn salsa!

Pulled Pork Sandwiches

Servings: 12
Cooking Time: 480 Minutes

Ingredients:

- One 7 to 8 pound pork butt, fat cap trimmed off
- 2 tablespoons vegetable oil
- Big Time BBQ Rub
- ½ cup apple juice
- 2 cups Dr. BBQ's Carolina Barbecue sauce
- 12 hamburger buns
- ½ cup salt
- ½ cup turbinado sugar
- ¼ cup granulated brown sugar
- 1 tablespoon granulated garlic
- 1 tablespoon granulated onion
- 2 tablespoons paprika
- 2 tablespoon chili powder
- 2 tablespoon freshly ground black pepper
- 2 teaspoons cayenne
- 1 tablespoon thyme leaves
- 1 tablespoon ground cumin
- 1 teaspoon ground nutmeg
- 1 c vinegar
- 2/3 cup catsup
- 2 teaspoons sugar
- 1 teaspoon salt
- 1 teaspoon Worcestershire
- ½ teaspoon red pepper flakes

Directions:

1. Rub the meat with the oil and then sprinkle liberally with the rub. Put in the refrigerator for at least a half hour and up to 12 hours.
2. Preheat the grill to 275°F using direct heat with a cast iron grate installed. Put the butt in the kamado grill and cook until the internal temperature is 160°F; this should take 6 to 8 hours. Lay out a big double piece of heavy duty aluminum foil and put the pork butt in the middle. As you begin to close up the package pour the apple juice over the top of the butt and then seal the package, taking care not to puncture it put it back in the kamado grill and cook until the meat reaches an internal temperature of 195°F; this should take another 2 to 3 hours.
3. Remove the package from the kamado grill to a baking sheet. Open the top of the foil to let the steam out and let it rest for ½ hour. Using heavy neoprene gloves or a pair of tongs and a fork transfer the meat to a big pan. It will be very tender and hard to handle. Discard the juices as they will be quite fatty. Shred the meat, discarding the fat and bones; it should just fall apart. Continue to pull the meat until it's shredded enough to make a sandwich. Add 1 cup of the sauce and mix well. Reserve the additional sauce for serving on the side. Serve on fluffy white buns topped with cole slaw.
4. Combine all ingredients, mix well, and store in an airtight container.
5. In a small saucepan mix together the vinegar, catsup, sugar, salt, Worcestershire and pepper flakes. Cook over low heat for 5 minutes stirring to blend.

Slow Roasted Pork Belly

Servings: 4

Cooking Time: 120 Minutes

Ingredients:
- 2 lbs. pork belly
- Kosher salt
- Your favorite herb rub (Rusty uses Pine Street Market Summer Spice)

Directions:
1. Preheat the grill to 225°F using direct heat with a cast iron grate installed.
2. Place the pork belly fat side up on the grill. Cook for 2 hours or until the internal temperature reaches 165°F.
3. Remove from the kamado grill and let rest for 10 minutes. Slice and serve. If you prefer crisper pork belly, sear the cooked pork belly in a cast iron skillet until crisp.

Stir-fried Cucumber And Pork With Golden Garlic

Servings: 2
Cooking Time: 5 Minutes

Ingredients:
- 1/2 cup (120 ml) peanut or vegetable oil
- 3 tbsp (45 ml) chopped garlic
- 12 ounces (340 g) lean pork shoulder or butt, cut into 1/4 inch (65 cm) thick bite-sized slices
- 1 1/2 tsp (8 ml) cornstarch
- 3 tsp (15 ml) soy sauce
- 1/4 tsp (1.5 ml) sugar
- 3/4 tsp (3.75 ml) salt
- 8 slices ginger, smashed
- 1 large English cucumber, ends trimmed, halved lengthwise and cut on the diagonal into 1/4 inch (65 cm) thick slices

Directions:
1. Preheat the grill to 600°F using direct heat with a cast iron grate installed. Once the kamado grill is steadily at this temperature, shut the bottom draft door and carefully open the lid.
2. Carbon Steel Wok, heat the pan until a bead of water vaporizes within 1 to 2 seconds of contact. Carefully add the oil and garlic and cook, stirring 30 seconds to 1 minute or until the garlic is light golden.
3. Remove the pan from the heat. Remove the garlic with a metal skimmer and put on a plate lined with paper towels. Carefully remove the oil from the woke and reserve. Wash the pan and dry it thoroughly.
4. In a shallow bowl combine the pork, cornstarch, 1 1/2 teaspoon (8 ml) of the soy sauce, sugar and 1/4 teaspoon (1.5 ml) of the salt. Ina small bowl combine the remaining 1 1/2 teaspoon (8 ml) soy sauce and 1 tablespoon (15 ml) cold water.
5. Again, heat the wok over high heat until a beat of water vaporizes within 1 to 2 seconds of contact. Swirl in 2 tablespoons (30 ml) of the reserved garlic oil, add the ginger slices; then, using a spatula, stir-fry 30 seconds or until the ginger is fragrant. Push the ginger to the sides of the wok, carefully add the pork, and spread it evenly in one layer in the pan.
6. Cook undisturbed 1 minute, letting the pork begin to sear. Then stir-fry 1 minute or until the pork is lightly browned but now cooked through. Add the cucumber and stir-fry 30 seconds or until well combined. Sprinkle on the remaining 1/2 tsp (2.5 ml) salt, swirl the reserved soy sauce mixture into the pan and stir-fry 1 minute or until the pork is just cooked and the cucumber begins to wilt. Stir in the reserved garlic.

Pork Curry

Servings: 6
Cooking Time: 20 Minutes

Ingredients:

- 2 pork tenderloins, about 3lb (1.4kg) in total, trimmed, silverskin removed, and cut into 2-in (.5-cm) pieces
- 3 cups cooked white rice
- naan bread, to serve (optional)
- for the marinade
- 4 dried red chile peppers
- 1/3 cup white vinegar
- 2 tsp ground cumin
- 1 tsp ground black pepper
- 1/2 tsp cinnamon
- 3 tsp ground cardamom
- 1 tsp ground cloves
- pinch of ground nutmeg
- 1 tsp grated fresh ginger
- 5 garlic cloves, peeled
- 1/2 cup olive oil
- 2 medium yellow onions, roughly chopped
- 1 tsp sugar
- kosher salt
- for the pickled mango
- 1/2 cup apple cider vinegar
- 1 tbsp sugar
- 1/2 tsp kosher salt
- 1 cup hot water
- 1 tbsp Vindaloo curry seasoning
- 1 ripe mango, peeled and sliced

Directions:

1. To make the marinade, in a small bowl, cover peppers with vinegar and let soak for 10 minutes. Transfer peppers and vinegar to a food processor, add remaining marinade ingredients, and blend until smooth. Transfer half the marinade to a resealable plastic bag. Reserve the remaining marinade and set aside.

2. Place pork pieces in the bag with the marinade and squeeze out any excess air. Refrigerate for at least 2 hours and up to 24 hours. Before grilling, remove from the fridge and bring to room temperature.

3. To make the pickled mango, in a small bowl, whisk together vinegar, sugar, and salt until sugar and salt have dissolved. Pack mango in a small jar and pour the vinegar mixture over top to cover. Let sit at room temperature for 1 hour.

4. Preheat the grill to 425°F (218°C) using direct heat with a cast iron grate installed and a dutch oven on the grate. Remove pork pieces from the marinade and place on the grate around the dutch oven (not inside). Close the grill lid and grill until the internal temperature reaches 140°F (60°C), about 8 to 12 minutes.

5. Transfer the grilled pork pieces to the dutch oven and add the cooked rice, reserved marinade, and pickled mango. (Discard pickling liquid or refrigerate in a sealable container for future use.) Cook until warmed through, about 5 to 7 minutes, stir occasionally. Serve immediately with warm naan (if desired).

Charlotte Pork Chops

Servings: 4

Cooking Time: 15 Minutes

Ingredients:
- 4 boneless pork chops, about ½ inch thick
- 4 medium yellow onions, halved and sliced thin
- 2 cloves garlic, crushed
- Vegetable oil
- BBQ rub
- 4 hamburger buns

Directions:
1. Preheat the grill to 400°F using direct heat with a cast iron grate installed.
2. Add the half cast iron griddle to one side to preheat. Season the chops with the barbecue rub. Add 1 to 2 tablespoons oil to the hot griddle and then add the onions. Season the onions with barbecue rub and sprinkle the garlic powder the top.
3. Cook for about 5 minutes tossing the onions occasionally. Add the pork chops and cook 3 to 4 minutes until golden broiwn. Flip and continue tossing the onions occasionally. Cook another 3 to 4 minutes until the chops are golden brown and have reached an internal temp of 150°F.
4. Remove the chops and onions from the grill. Place a chop on each bun and top with ¼ of the onions.

Pulled Pork Nachos With Fire-roasted Salsa

Servings: 6

Cooking Time: 7 Minutes

Ingredients:
- 1 lb. pulled pork
- 1 bag tortilla chips
- 1 can black beans, strained
- 2 cups shredded cheddar cheese
- 1 cup guacamole
- 1 cup sour cream
- ½ cup pickled jalapenos
- ¼ cup minced cilantro
- 1 cup cheese dip
- 6 tomatoes
- 4 jalapeño peppers
- 8 cloves garlic
- 1 red onion
- 3 scallions
- ¼ cup chopped cilantro
- 2 tbsp lime juice
- ½ tbsp black pepper
- 2 tbsp kosher salt
- 1 tbsp Ancho Chile & Coffee Seasoning
- 1 tbsp chili powder
- 1 tbsp cumin

Directions:
1. Preheat the grill to 400°F using direct heat with a cast iron grate installed.
2. Add the tortilla chips to the cast iron skillet and top with pulled pork, beans, cheese and pickled jalapenos. Place on the kamado grill for 5-7 minutes or until the shredded cheese has melted. While the nachos are on the grill, add cheese dip to the saucepot and place in the kamado grill to heat.
3. Remove nachos and cheese dip from the grill. Pour the cheese dip all over the nachos, top with guacamole, sour cream and fire-roasted salsa. Garnish with cilantro. Enjoy!
4. Place the whole tomatoes, jalapenos, onion, and scallions directly on the grid and grill until there are char marks. Remove from the kamado grill and cut all of the vegetables into smaller pieces and put in the blender. If a milder salsa is desired remove the seeds from the jalapeno peppers. Add the garlic, lime juice, cilantro, pepper, salt, Ancho Chili & Coffee Seasoning, chili powder and cumin to the blender. Blend until desired texture. Add more salt to taste.

Smoked Spicy Korean Spare Ribs

Servings: 12

Cooking Time: 300 Minutes

Ingredients:
- 2 racks pork spareribs, membranes removed
- Sweet and Smoky Seasoning
- 1 green onion, sliced
- 1 red jalapeño pepper, sliced
- ½ cup gochujang
- ¼ cup hoisin sauce
- ¼ cup ketchup
- ¼ cup honey
- ¼ cup soy sauce
- ¼ cup Korean rice wine
- 1 tbsp unseasoned rice vinegar
- 2" piece fresh ginger, finely gated
- 3 cloves of finely grated garlic
- 1 tbsp ground white pepper

Directions:
1. Preheat the grill to 250°F using direct heat with a cast iron grate installed.
2. Trim the excess fat from the ribs and cover in the Sweet and Smoky Seasoning.
3. Put in the ribs bone side down in the grill. After cooking for 3 hours glaze with Korean BBQ sauce. Cook for another hour.
4. Raise the temperature to 300° and glaze the ribs with the Korean BBQ sauce. Place back in the kamado grill for an hour.
5. When the meat pulls from the bone it is time to remove from the grill. Garnish with the green onion and jalapeño pepper. Enjoy!
6. Mix all the Korean BBQ ingredients together and set in the refrigerator.

Whole Roasted Chicken With Garlic & Fresh Herb Butter

Servings: 6
Cooking Time: 90 Minutes

Ingredients:
- 1 whole chicken, about 5lb (2.3kg) in total
- for the brine
- 1/2 cup kosher salt
- 1/2 cup packed light brown sugar
- 3 tbsp pickling spice
- 6 cups hot water
- for the butter
- 3 heads of garlic, separated into peeled cloves
- 1 tbsp olive oil
- 8 tbsp unsalted butter, softened
- 3/4 cup chopped mixed fresh herbs, such as thyme, rosemary, and oregano
- 5 tsp sherry vinegar
- 2 tbsp kosher salt

Directions:
1. To make the brine, in a large bowl, whisk together all the brine ingredients until salt and sugar have dissolved. Add ice cubes until the liquid is no longer hot. Place chicken in a resealable plastic bag and add brine to cover. (Any extra brine can be refrigerated and saved for a later use.) Refrigerate for 6 to 24 hours.
2. Preheat the grill to 350°F (177°C) using indirect heat with a standard grate installed. Wrap garlic and oil in aluminum foil, place on the grate, close the lid, and cook for 30 minutes. Remove garlic from the grill and roughly chop.
3. To make the butter, in a stand mixer, combine butter, herbs, vinegar, salt, and garlic.
4. Remove chicken from the brine and pat dry with paper towels. Loosen the skin and allow chicken to come to room temperature. Rub butter under the skin and on top of the skin. Reserve remaining butter for basting.
5. Place chicken in a roasting pan breast side up and set the pan on the grate. Close the grill lid and roast until chicken reaches an internal temperature of 170°F (77°C), about 40 to 60 minutes. Baste with more butter every 20 minutes.
6. Remove chicken from the grill, let rest for 10 to 15 minutes, and cut into quarters or carve. Serve with any remaining butter.

Duck & Potatoes

Servings: 12
Cooking Time: 90 Minutes

Ingredients:

- 8 duck breasts, about 4lb (1.8kg) in total
- 8 mild green chile peppers
- 4 tbsp olive oil
- kosher salt and freshly ground black pepper
- 1 large white onion, chopped
- 1 tbsp cumin seeds
- 15 tomatillos, husked, rinsed, and cut into wedges
- 1 cup chicken stock
- 2 tsp dried oregano
- 1lb (450g) Yukon Gold potatoes, peeled and cut into cubes
- chopped fresh cilantro, to garnish
- for the brine
- 1/2 cup kosher salt
- 1/2 cup packed light brown sugar
- 3 tbsp pickling spice
- 6 cups hot water
- for the salsa verde
- 2 cups chicken stock
- 5 tomatillos, husked, rinsed, and cut into wedges
- 1 bunch of scallions, coarsely chopped
- 1 1/2 cups packed fresh cilantro leaves and tender stems
- 6 garlic cloves, peeled

Directions:

1. To make the brine, in a medium bowl, whisk together salt, brown sugar, pickling spice, and water until salt and sugar have dissolved. Add ice cubes a few at a time until the liquid is no longer hot. Place duck breasts in a resealable plastic bag and add brine to cover. (Any extra brine can be refrigerated and saved for a later use.) Refrigerate for 1 hour.
2. Preheat the grill to 350°F (177°C) using direct heat with a cast iron grate installed and a dutch oven on the grate. Place green chiles on the grate around the dutch oven, close the grill lid, and grill until charred, about 7 to 10 minutes. Remove from the grill, seed, dice, and set aside.
3. In the hot dutch oven, heat oil until shimmering. Remove duck from the brine, pat dry with paper towels, and slice into thin strips. Sprinkle duck with salt and pepper to taste. Working in two batches, add duck to the dutch oven. Leave the lid off the dutch oven, close the grill lid, and cook until browned, about 4 minutes per batch, turning occasionally. Using a slotted spoon, transfer duck to a serving bowl, retaining 1 tbsp fat.
4. Add onion to the dutch oven and sauté until soft, about 5 minutes. Add cumin seeds and cook until onion is golden and cumin is toasted, about 2 minutes. Add tomatillos and cook until tender and browned in spots, about 8 minutes, stirring occasionally.
5. To make the salsa verde, in a blender or food processor, purée all the salsa ingredients until smooth. Return duck and any juices to the dutch oven. Add 2 cups salsa verde, chicken stock, chiles, and oregano. Place the lid on the dutch oven, close the grill lid, and simmer until duck is tender, about 2 hours.
6. Add potatoes to the dutch oven. Replace the lid, close the grill lid, and simmer until potatoes are tender, about 30 minutes. Stir in remaining salsa verde and bring to a simmer. Thin with more stock (if desired), and season with salt and pepper to taste. Sprinkle with cilantro before serving.

Potato Salad With Bacon

Servings: 6
Cooking Time: 20 Minutes

Ingredients:
- 6 slices bacon, thick-cut, cooked until crisp, then coarsely crumbled
- 2 pounds red new potatoes, (golf-ball size), scrubbed and poked with a fork
- 2 tablespoons extra-virgin olive oil
- 4 green onions, including green tops, cut crosswise into thin rounds
- ¼ cup extra-virgin olive oil
- 1 tablespoon apple cider vinegar
- 1 large clove garlic, minced
- 2 tablespoons fresh parsley, minced
- 1 teaspoon kosher salt
- ½ teaspoon sugar
- 1 teaspoon freshly ground black pepper

Directions:
1. Preheat the grill to 350°F using direct heat with a cast iron grate installed.
2. In a medium bowl, toss potatoes with olive oil until well coated. Arrange potatoes around outer edges of cooking grid. Grill until tender when pierced with a knife, about 20 minutes.
3. While potatoes are grilling, put green onions and bacon in a large bowl, and make dressing. Combine olive oil, vinegar, garlic, parsley, salt, sugar and pepper in a small bowl; set aside.
4. When potatoes are tender, transfer to a cutting board and cool for 5 minutes. Cut potatoes in half and add to bacon and onions in the bowl. Stir dressing to combine and pour over potatoes. Gently toss to thoroughly combine. Serve immediately.
5. The potato salad can be made up to 2 hours prior to serving. Cover and set aside at room temperature.

Spanish Pork Tenderloins

Servings: 6
Cooking Time: 15 Minutes

Ingredients:
- 1 pound pork tenderloin
- 2 tsp olive oil
- 3/4 tsp smoked sweet paprika (pimenton)
- 1/2 tsp garlic powder
- 1/4 tsp salt
- 1/4 tsp ground cumin
- 1 cup Romesco Sauce

Directions:
1. In a blender, combine all ingredients and blend until smooth. Set aside. The sauce can be made up to 3 days in advance.
2. Combine rub ingredients.
3. Brush tenderloins with olive oil and sprinkle liberally with the rub. Set aside.
4. Grilling:
5. Preheat the grill to 450°F using direct heat with a cast iron grate installed.
6. Place the tenderloins on the grid and close the dome for 10 minutes.
7. Flip the tenderloins and cook another 10 minutes or until the internal temperature reaches 150°F.
8. Remove from the grill and allow to rest for 10 minutes before slicing and serving with the Romesco sauce.

Smoked Spareribs

Servings: 8
Cooking Time: 300 Minutes

Ingredients:
- 2 racks spareribs, peeled
- 4 tablespoons paprika
- 4 tablespoons kosher salt
- 4 tablespoons granulated garlic
- 4 tablespoons sugar
- 2 tablespoon sugar in the raw
- 2 tablespoon chile powder
- 2 tablespoon black pepper
- 2 tablespoon onion powder
- 2 tablespoon dried oregano
- 2 tablespoon dried thyme
- ½ cup sugar
- 1 teaspoon dried oregano
- ½ teaspoon dried thyme
- 1 teaspoon granulated garlic
- 2 teaspoon kosher salt
- 1 teaspoon black pepper
- ½ cup white vinegar
- 1 cup molasses
- 1 cup Red Gold Tomato Ketchup or Mama Selita's Jalapeno Ketchup
- ¾ cup yellow mustard
- 1 teaspoon cayenne pepper
- Cherry wood chunks, for smoking, if desired

Directions:
1. Combine all of the ingredients for the rub. Evenly rub the ribs, wrap them in foil refrigerate them overnight.
2. Preheat the grill to 245°F using direct heat with a cast iron grate installed.
3. Smoke the ribs for 3 hours, wrap them in foil, return to the kamado grill and cook for another 2 hours. Remove from the kamado grill after 2 hours, and rest for 1 more.
4. Combine all of the ingredients for the BBQ sauce and bring to a simmer. Remove from the heat and base the ribs with the sauce before serving.

Twice-smoked Ham

Servings: 16
Cooking Time: 210 Minutes

Ingredients:

- 18lb (8kg) bone-in whole or spiral-cut smoked ham, at room temperature
- 1 cup water
- for the glaze
- 1 cup sugar
- 2 tbsp water
- 1 tbsp fennel seeds
- 1 tbsp coriander seeds
- 4 star anise pods
- 4 bay leaves
- 2 cinnamon sticks
- 2 garlic cloves
- 1-in (2.5-cm) piece fresh ginger, thinly sliced
- 1 dried red chile pepper
- 1 tsp finely grated orange zest
- 2 cups bourbon
- 2 tbsp low-sodium soy sauce
- 2 tbsp honey
- to smoke
- hickory or apple wood chunks

Directions:

1. Preheat the grill to 300°F (149°C) using indirect heat. Once hot, add the wood chunks and install the heat deflector and a standard grate. Place the precooked ham in a large roasting pan (a disposable aluminum pan works well) and add water. Place the pan on the grate, close the lid, and smoke until an instant-read thermometer inserted in the thickest part of the meat reads 120°F (49°C), about 2 hours and 45 minutes, basting occasionally with any accumulated juices.
2. To make the glaze, in a medium saucepan, combine sugar and water, and place the pan on the stovetop over medium-high heat. Cook until a light golden syrup forms, about 8 to 10 minutes, swirling the pan occasionally.
3. Remove from the heat and quickly add fennel seeds, coriander seeds, star anise, bay leaves, cinnamon, garlic, ginger, chile pepper, and orange zest. Let sit until fragrant, about 20 seconds. Carefully add the bourbon, soy sauce, and honey. Return the glaze to medium heat and bring to a simmer until slightly thickened, about 10 minutes, stirring occasionally.
4. Once ham reaches 120°F (49°C), brush it with the glaze. Continue smoking until the top is lightly caramelized, about 30 minutes more, brushing with glaze every 10 minutes.
5. Transfer ham to a platter and let rest for 15 minutes. Skim the fat from the pan and transfer the juices to a bowl. Slice and serve with the warm pan juices.

Barbecue Pork Shoulder

Servings: 4
Cooking Time: 840 Minutes

Ingredients:
- 1 (6-8 lb) pork shoulder
- 2 cups East Carolina Barbecue Sauce
- 1 cup Basic BBQ Rub
- 2 cups wood chips, soaked in water for a minimum of 1 hour (any wood is great for this recipe)

Directions:
1. Score the skin of pork shoulder with a knife, cutting only through the skin, not the meat.
2. Liberally sprinkle the pork with BBQ Rub, cover tightly in an aluminum pan and refrigerate 4 hours or up to overnight.
3. Remove the pork shoulder from the refrigerator 1 hour before cooking.
4. Grilling:
5. Preheat the grill to 225°F using direct heat with a cast iron grate installed. Add the drained wood chips to the coals and place the plate setter and grid inside the grill.
6. Place the pork shoulder on the grid and close the dome.
7. The grill will hold its heat at this temperature for up to 18 hours, so you can literally set it and forget it.
8. After 12 hours, check the internal temperature of the roast. It will be a deep mahogany color, but if the temperature has been maintained, it will not be burned or dried out. When the internal temperature reaches 200°F, carefully remove the roast with two forks.
9. Gently pull the meat apart and sprinkle with East Carolina Barbecue Sauce. Serve with additional sauce.

Turkey Bacon Dogs

Servings: 8
Cooking Time: 20 Minutes

Ingredients:
- 8 Nature's Own 100% Whole Wheat Hot Dog Rolls
- 1 package (16 ounces) Butterball Bun Size Premium Turkey Franks
- 8 slices Butterball Turkey Bacon
- 1/2 to 3/4 cup shredded Cheddar or Monterey Jack cheese
- Salsa (medium or hot)
- Pickled jalapeño pepper slices (optional)
- Sour cream (optional)

Directions:
1. Preheat the grill to 500°F using direct heat with a cast iron grate installed.
2. Spray cold grate of grill with cooking spray. Wrap each turkey frank with 1 slice turkey bacon. Grill franks, turning frequently, until bacon is crisp.
3. Place franks in hot dog rolls. Immediately sprinkle with cheese. Serve with salsa and if desired, jalapeno pepper slices and sour cream.

Dr. Bbq's Spare Rib Surprise

Servings: 4
Cooking Time: 195 Minutes

Ingredients:
- 2 slabs (about 4 lb/1.8 kg each) whole spareribs
- 1 recipe Secret Apple Juice Injection
- 1 cup (220 g) barbecue rub such as Barbecue Rub #34 1/2 cup (120 ml) apple juice
- 1 1/2 cups (360 ml) apple juice
- 1/4 cup (50 g) Sugar In The Raw or other raw sugar
- 1 tbsp Morton's Kosher Salt
- 2 tbsp yellow mustard
- 2 tbsp soy sauce
- 1/2 tsp cayenne
- 1/4 cup (60 g) Morton's Kosher Salt
- 1/4 cup (50 g) packed brown sugar
- 2 tbsp paprika
- 1 tbsp chili powder
- 1 tbsp granulated onion
- 1 tsp granulated garlic
- 2 tsp black pepper

Directions:
1. A half hour before you plan to cook, peel the membrane off the back of the ribs and cut the flap of meat across the bone side off. Trim any excess fat.
2. Using the Injector, inject the ribs in between the bones from both ends until all of the injection liquid has been used up. Season the ribs liberally on both sides with the rub. Refrigerate them until needed.
3. Preheat the grill to 275°F using direct heat with a cast iron grate installed. Place the ribs meaty-side up on the kamado grill and close the dome. Cook them for 2 hours. Flip the ribs over and cook them for another hour.
4. Lay out two large double-thick sheets of heavy-duty aluminum foil. Lay a slab of ribs on each, meaty-side up. As you begin to fold the foil up around the ribs, add 1/4 cup (60 ml) of the apple juice to the bottom of each package. Continue folding the foil up around the ribs, closing it into a package. Return the rib packets to the kamado grill for 1 hour, or until the ribs are tender when poked with a toothpick.
5. Remove the ribs from the foil and place them back on the kamado grill meaty-side up. Cook them for 15 minutes more, until the ribs are firmed up. Place the ribs meaty-side down on a cutting board and use a sharp knife to cut through the slab completely at each rib. To serve, flip the ribs over, reconstructing the slabs on a platter.
6. In a medium bowl, combine the apple juice, raw sugar, salt, mustard, soy sauce, and cayenne. With a fork or whisk, mix everything until well blended. Cover and refrigerate the mixture for up to 1 week.
7. In a small bowl, combine the salt, brown sugar, paprika, chili powder, granulated onion, granulated garlic, and pepper. Mix them well until fully blended. Store in an airtight container in a cool dry place for up to 2 months.

Dutch Oven Pork Roast

Servings: 6
Cooking Time: 75 Minutes

Ingredients:
- 1 3-4 lb boneless pork loin roast
- 2 lbs small potatoes (we like reds or Yukon golds)
- 1 lb parsnips, peeled and cut into 1 inch chunks
- 1 Tablespoon fresh thyme
- Salt and Pepper
- 1/4 cup brown mustard
- 2 Tablespoons Worcestershire sauce
- 2 Tablespoons olive oil

Directions:
1. In a cold dutch oven, toss vegetables with olive oil and a sprinkling of salt and pepper.
2. In a small bowl, combine mustard, Worcestershire, and thyme. Paint all over the loin roast.
3. Place the roast on top of the vegetables.
4. Grilling:
5. Preheat the grill to 425°F using direct heat with a cast iron grate installed.
6. Cover the dutch oven and place on the waiting grill.
7. Lower the dome for 1 hour to 1 hour and 15 minutes or until the internal temperature of the roast reaches 155°F
8. Remove the dutch oven from the grill, remove the pork and set aside to rest for 20 minutes before carving. Recover the dutch oven to keep the vegetables warm in the meantime.
9. Serve warm.

SIDES

Alligator Eggs

Servings: 6
Cooking Time: 10 Minutes

Ingredients:
- 8 ounces cream cheese, softened
- 1 cup sharp cheddar cheese
- 12 thin slices bacon
- 6 jalapeños

Directions:
1. Slice jalapeños in half and remove seeds. Set aside.
2. In a small bowl, combine cheddar cheese and cream cheese until mixed.
3. Stuff 2 Tablespoon of the cream cheese mixture into each jalapeño half.
4. Wrap each jalapeño half in one strip of bacon, securing with a toothpick.
5. Grilling:
6. Preheat the grill to 425°F using direct heat with a cast iron grate installed.
7. Place the alligator eggs directly on the grid and close the dome for 10 minutes or until the bacon is crisp. Serve immediately.

Wood-plank Loaded Mashed Potatoes

Servings: 16
Cooking Time: 50 Minutes

Ingredients:
- 1lb (450g) red potatoes
- 1lb (450g) Yukon Gold potatoes
- 1 tbsp kosher salt, plus 1 tsp
- 2 strips bacon, diced
- 2 tbsp unsalted butter
- ¼ cup sour cream
- ¼ cup heavy cream
- 4oz (113g) shredded Cheddar cheese, plus more for topping
- 4 scallions, thinly sliced, plus more for topping
- freshly ground black pepper

Directions:

1. Place a 4 x 9in (10 x 23cm) cedar wood plank in a baking dish, cover with cold water, and place heavy cans or stones on the plank to keep it submerged. Soak for 1 to 2 hours.

2. Place red potatoes and Yukon Gold potatoes in a large stockpot and add cold water to cover by several inches. Place the pot on the stovetop over high heat, add 1 tsp salt, and bring to a boil. Reduce to a simmer, cover, and cook until potatoes are fork tender, about 25 minutes. Drain potatoes, reserving 1 cup cooking water.

3. Preheat the grill to 350°F (177°C) using direct heat with a standard grate installed and a cast iron skillet on the grate. Add bacon to the hot skillet, and cook until bacon is crisp and the fat has rendered, about 10 to 15 minutes, stirring occasionally. Transfer the cooked bacon pieces to a plate lined with a paper towel.

4. In a large bowl, combine potatoes, butter, sour cream, heavy cream, Cheddar cheese, scallions, bacon, and 1 tbsp salt. Mash with a potato masher until potatoes have broken down and cheese and sour cream are fully incorporated. If potatoes are too stiff, add some of the reserved cooking water.

5. Place the soaked plank on the grate and allow it to heat for 2 to 5 minutes, then flip it over. Scoop the mashed potatoes onto the heated side of the plank. Top the potatoes with a little Cheddar cheese, close the lid, and cook until cheese has melted and potatoes have browned slightly, about 7 to 10 minutes. Remove potatoes from the grill, sprinkle with scallions, and serve immediately.

Grilled Watermelon Salad

Servings: 6
Cooking Time: 6 Minutes

Ingredients:
- 4 medium cucumbers, about 1lb (450g) in total, divided
- 3lb (1.4kg) watermelon, rind removed and cut into thick slices
- 3 garlic cloves, peeled
- 1 1/2 cups plain Greek yogurt
- 2/3 cup chopped mint, divided
- 3/4 tsp kosher salt
- 2 tbsp fresh lime juice
- flaky sea salt, to serve

Directions:
1. Preheat the grill to 500°F (260°C) using direct heat with a cast iron grate installed. Peel 2 cucumbers and halve them lengthwise. Place the halved cucumbers and watermelon slices on the grate, close the lid, and grill until grill marks form, about 2 to 3 minutes per side.
2. Using a chef's knife, finely chop garlic and sprinkle with a pinch of salt. Using the flat of the blade, crush the chopped garlic, scrape into a pile, and crush again, repeating until a paste forms. Transfer to a medium bowl.
3. To make the tzatziki sauce, peel the remaining 2 cucumbers, halve lengthwise, and seed. Coarsely grate into the bowl with the garlic paste. Stir in yogurt, 1/3 cup mint, and salt.
4. Cut the watermelon into bite-sized pieces, and cut the grilled cucumber crosswise into 1/3-in (.75-cm) slices. Place cucumber and watermelon in a large bowl, toss with lime juice and the remaining 1/3 cup mint, and sprinkle with sea salt. Spoon the tzatziki sauce over top to serve.

Grilled Onions

Servings: 4
Cooking Time: 60 Minutes

Ingredients:
- 4 large sweet onions
- 4 Tablespoons butter
- 1 tsp salt
- 1/2 tsp pepper

Directions:
1. Remove the stem end of each onion and peel the skin away.
2. With a melon baller, remove 1 inch of the core of the onion being careful not to disturb the root end.
3. Place 1 Tablespoon of butter, 1/4 tsp salt, and 1/8 tsp pepper into each onion.
4. Grilling:
5. Wrap the onions in aluminum foil and place on a 225°F grill for 1 hour with the dome closed.
6. Unwrap the onions and serve warm.

Grilled Sweet Potatoes

Servings: 12
Cooking Time: 20 Minutes

Ingredients:
- 5 tbsp olive oil
- 5 tbsp pure maple syrup
- 3 tbsp kosher salt
- 6 garlic cloves, minced, plus more to serve
- 2 tsp finely chopped fresh thyme leaves
- 1/4 tsp crushed red pepper flakes
- 6 large sweet potatoes, about 3lb (1.4kg) in total, peeled and cut into thick wedges
- 2 tbsp finely chopped fresh flat-leaf parsley

Directions:
1. Preheat the grill to 400°F using direct heat with a cast iron grate installed.
2. In a large bowl, whisk together oil, syrup, salt, garlic, thyme, and red pepper flakes. Add potatoes and toss to coat. Season with more salt (if desired).
3. Place wedges on the grate, being sure to shake off excess liquid, close the lid, and grill until lightly golden brown and just cooked through, about 15 to 20 minutes, turning often.
4. Transfer to a serving bowl and immediately toss with parsley and more minced garlic (if desired). Season with salt to taste.

Grilled Lemon Garlic Zucchini

Servings: 6
Cooking Time: 5 Minutes

Ingredients:
- 4 zucchini, sliced lengthwise into 1/2 inch slices
- 1/4 cup butter, softened
- 2 tsp parsley, chopped
- 3 cloves garlic, minced
- The zest and juice of 1 lemon

Directions:
1. In a small dish, combine butter, parsley, garlic, lemon zest, and lemon juice.
2. Liberally brush each zucchini slice with the butter mixture.
3. Grilling:
4. Place the zucchini on a 500°F grill and close the dome for 3 minutes.
5. Flip the zucchini and recover with the dome for an additional 2 minutes.
6. Drizzle remaining butter on top of zucchini as it comes off the grill. Serve warm.

Wood-plank Stuffed Tomatoes

Servings: 8
Cooking Time: 20 Minutes

Ingredients:

- 4 beefsteak tomatoes
- 1 cup chopped fresh flat-leaf parsley
- 3/4 cup Italian-style breadcrumbs
- 1 cup grated provolone
- 1/4 tsp ground black pepper
- 1 tsp unsalted butter, softened
- 2 tbsp extra virgin olive oil

Directions:

1. Place a 4 x 9in (10 x 23cm) wood plank in a baking dish, cover with cold water, and place heavy cans or stones on the plank to keep it submerged. Soak for 1 to 2 hours.
2. Preheat the grill to 425°F (218°C) using indirect heat with a standard grate installed. Place the wood plank on the grate.
3. Cut tomatoes in half horizontally and hollow out the insides, discarding the seeds and reserving the pulp. Chop the reserved pulp and place in a medium bowl. Add parsley, breadcrumbs, provolone, and pepper, and mix gently to combine. Fill each tomato half with the breadcrumb mixture and top with a drizzle of oil.
4. Flip the plank over, spread butter on the hot side, and arrange tomatoes cut side up on the plank. Place the plank on the grate, close the lid, and cook until the tops are browned and the tomatoes are soft, about 20 minutes. Remove tomatoes from the grill and serve immediately.

Parmesan Zucchini Spears

Servings: 4
Cooking Time: 10 Minutes

Ingredients:

- 4 zucchini, cut in half, then cut into quarters lengthwise
- 1/2 cup parmesan, grated
- 1 tsp Italian seasoning
- 1/2 tsp garlic powder
- Salt and Pepper to taste
- Olive oil for brushing

Directions:

1. Brush each zucchini spear with olive oil and season with salt and pepper.
2. In a small bowl, combine Italian seasoning, garlic powder, and parmesan.
3. Place zucchini spears on a small sheet tray and sprinkle the parmesan over each spear.
4. Grilling:
5. Place the sheet tray on the grid of a 500°F grill.
6. Close the dome and cook for 10 minutes or until the parmesan is golden brown. Serve warm.

Soba Noodle Bowl

Servings: 6
Cooking Time: 30 Minutes

Ingredients:
- 12oz (28g) soba noodles
- 4 scallions
- 2 red bell peppers, left whole
- 1 carrot, peeled
- 1/2 head of napa cabbage
- 1/4 cup chopped hazelnuts
- chopped fresh cilantro, to garnish
- for the sauce
- 1/2 cup peanut butter
- 1/4 cup soy sauce
- 1/3 cup warm water
- 2 tbsp ground ginger
- 1 garlic clove
- 2 tbsp white wine vinegar
- 1 1/2 tsp honey
- 1 tsp crushed red pepper flakes

Directions:
1. To make the sauce, combine all the sauce ingredients in a blender and purée until smooth. Set aside. (Sauce can be made in advance. Refrigerate in an airtight container and use within 1 week.)
2. Cook the pasta according to the package directions until cooked but still firm to the bite. Drain and rinse well under cold water. Set aside.
3. Preheat the grill to 400°F (204°C) using direct heat with a cast iron grate installed and a cast iron skillet on the grate. Place scallions, peppers, carrot, and napa cabbage around the skillet, close the lid, and grill until beginning to soften and char, about 7 to 10 minutes. Slice peppers and carrots thinly, and shred cabbage.
4. Add the vegetables and noodles to the hot skillet, and stir to combine. Add the sauce, and stir until well incorporated and heated through, about 3 to 4 minutes.
5. Remove the skillet from the grill and top noodles with hazelnuts and cilantro. Serve immediately.

Dutch Oven Black Beans

Servings: 6
Cooking Time: 40 Minutes

Ingredients:
- 1 medium yellow onion, peeled and halved
- 1 green bell pepper, left whole
- 2 x 15oz (425g) cans black beans with liquid or 3 cups cooked black beans
- 2 garlic cloves, minced
- 1 tsp ground cumin
- 1/2 tsp dried oregano
- 1/2 tsp kosher salt
- 1 tsp red wine vinegar
- 1 bunch of fresh cilantro, chopped

Directions:
1. Preheat the grill to 350°F using direct heat with a cast iron grate installed and a dutch oven on the grate. Arrange onions and pepper on the grate around the dutch oven, close the grill lid, and grill until beginning to soften and char, about 5 to 7 minutes. Transfer the vegetables to a cutting board and chop.
2. Add 1/8 cup bean liquid to the dutch oven. Add onion, pepper, and garlic, close the grill lid, and sauté until soft, about 2 minutes. Add beans with the remaining liquid. Stir in cumin, oregano, and salt. Cover the dutch oven with its lid and close the grill lid. Simmer for 15 to 30 minutes.
3. Remove the dutch oven from the grill and stir in the vinegar and cilantro, reserving a bit to sprinkle over top. Serve immediately.

Bacon Wrapped Pineapple

Servings: 6
Cooking Time: 10 Minutes

Ingredients:
- 1 cup Classic Texas Barbecue Sauce
- 1 lb bacon, cut into 4 inch strips
- 1 pineapple cut into 2 inch cubes

Directions:
1. Wrap each pineapple piece with a 4 inch strip of bacon and secure with a toothpick.
2. Grilling:
3. Preheat the grill to 425°F using direct heat with a cast iron grate installed and place on the grid. Close the dome for 8 minutes or until the bacon is crispy.
4. Brush each pineapple chunk with barbecue sauce and close the dome for another 2 minutes.
5. Serve warm with additional barbecue sauce for dipping.

Corn, Bacon & Chorizo Hash

Servings: 4
Cooking Time: 40 Minutes

Ingredients:
- 4 ears of corn, shucked
- 2 Fresno peppers
- 1lb (450g) new potatoes, halved if large
- 8oz (225g) chorizo sausage, casings removed
- 8oz (225g) thick-cut bacon, diced
- 2 shallots, finely diced
- kosher salt and freshly ground black pepper

Directions:
1. Preheat the grill to 350°F using indirect heat with a cast iron grate installed and a cast iron skillet on the grate. Place corn, peppers, and potatoes on the grate around the skillet, close the grill lid, and grill until beginning to soften and char, about 6 to 10 minutes. (Peppers and corn cook more quickly than the potatoes.) Remove the vegetables from the grill. Cut the kernels from the cobs, seed and dice the peppers, and dice the potatoes. Set aside.
2. In the hot skillet, cook chorizo for 10 minutes, stirring once or twice. Transfer the cooked chorizo to a platter and set aside. Return the skillet to the grill, add bacon, close the grill lid, and cook until crisp and the fat has rendered, about 10 minutes. Drain the bacon grease, reserving 1 tbsp in the skillet along with the cooked bacon, and return the skillet to the grill.
3. Add shallots to the skillet, close the grill lid, and sauté until soft and translucent, about 2 minutes. Add corn kernels, potatoes, and chorizo, close the grill lid, and sauté for 5 to 7 minutes more. Add half the diced peppers and season with salt and pepper. Taste to check the spice level before adding the remaining diced peppers. Stir and cook for 1 minute more. Remove the hash from the grill and serve immediately.

Grilled Polenta

Servings: 8
Cooking Time: 5 Minutes

Ingredients:
- 3 cups water
- 3/4 cups parmesan cheese, grated
- 2 Tablespoons butter
- 1 tsp fresh thyme, chopped
- 1 1/2 cups quick cooking polenta
- 2 tsp salt
- 1 tsp pepper
- Olive oil for brushing

Directions:
1. In a large pot, bring water to a boil with the salt.
2. Slowly whisk in polenta and season with pepper.
3. Continue to whisk until polenta becomes firm.
4. Stir in parmesan and thyme.
5. Pour polenta into a buttered 10 inch springform pan and refrigerate for 1 1/2 - 2 hours or until the polenta is firm.
6. Remove the polenta from the springform pan and slice into 8 pieces.
7. Grilling:
8. Brush both sides with olive oil and place on a 400°F grill.
9. Close the dome and cook for 2 minutes.
10. Turn the polenta, close the dome and continue to cook for another 2 minutes. Serve warm.

Mac And Cheese

Servings: 6
Cooking Time: 60 Minutes

Ingredients:
- 1 lb smoked cheddar cheese, shredded, divided
- 1/4 cup butter
- 2 eggs
- 1/2 lb elbow macaroni
- 3/4 cups evaporated milk
- 1/4 cup Panko breadcrumbs
- 1 tsp salt
- 3/4 tsp dry mustard

Directions:
1. In a large pot of boiling, salted water cook the macaroni according to package directions and drain.
2. In a separate bowl, whisk together the eggs, milk, hot sauce, salt, pepper, and mustard.
3. Grilling:
4. Preheat the grill to 350°F using direct heat with a cast iron grate installed with the dutch oven on the grid.
5. Melt the butter in the dutch oven and place macaroni in the pot. Toss to coat.
6. Stir the egg and milk mixture into the pasta and add half of the cheese.
7. Continuously stir the mac and cheese for 3 minutes or until creamy.
8. Top with remaining cheese and Panko breadcrumbs.
9. Cover the dutch oven, lower the dome, and cook for 20-25 minutes.
10. Serve immediately.

Breakfast Casserole

Servings: 6
Cooking Time: 40 Minutes

Ingredients:
- 1 lb bulk pork breakfast sausage
- 1 (16 oz) bag of frozen O'Brien style hash browns
- 1 dozen eggs, beaten
- 1/4 cup grated onion
- 1/4 tsp black pepper
- Hot sauce for garnish

Directions:
1. Preheat the grill to 350°F using direct heat with a cast iron grate installed with the dutch oven on the grid.
2. Brown sausage with onion in the dutch oven.
3. Add hash browns and stir to combine.
4. Add eggs and cover.
5. Lower the dome for 15 minutes or until the eggs are just cooked through.
6. Serve the casserole with hot sauce for garnish.

Corn & Poblano Pudding

Servings: 8
Cooking Time: 30 Minutes

Ingredients:
- vegetable oil, for greasing
- 4 ears of sweet corn, shucked
- 1 poblano pepper, left whole
- 4 large eggs
- 1 cup whole milk
- 1/2 tsp kosher salt
- 1/4 tsp ground nutmeg
- 1/4 tsp ground cayenne pepper
- 2oz (55g) shredded Cheddar cheese

Directions:

1. Preheat the grill to 350°F (177°C) using indirect heat with a standard grate installed. Grease a cast iron skillet with oil.

2. Place corn and pepper on the grate, positioning them around the edges, close the lid, and grill until beginning to soften and char, about 10 minutes. Transfer the vegetables to a cutting board, cut the kernels from the cobs, and seed and dice the pepper.

3. In a large bowl, whisk together eggs, milk, salt, nutmeg, cayenne, and cheese until well combined. Stir in corn kernels and pepper. Pour the mixture into the greased dish and place on the grate. Close the lid and bake until a knife inserted halfway between the center and the outer edge comes out clean, about 20 minutes. Remove the pudding from the grill and serve warm or at room temperature.

Grilled Endive Salad

Servings: 6
Cooking Time: 2 Minutes

Ingredients:
- 2 cups frisee
- 1/2 cup pecan halves
- 1/4 cup dried cranberries
- 1/4 cup crumbled bacon
- 2 heads endive
- 1 bunch spinach, cleaned and stems removed
- 1/4 cup olive oil
- 2 Tablespoons Dijon Mustard
- 1 Tablespoon honey
- 1 shallot, finely minced
- The juice of 1 lemon
- Kosher salt and fresh cracked pepper to taste

Directions:
1. In a large bowl, combine dressing ingredients. Set aside.
2. Grilling:
3. Split endive down the middle, lengthwise and preheat the grill to 425°F using direct heat with a cast iron grate installed.
4. Remove the endive and slice into half rounds.
5. Toss shredded frisee, sliced endive, spinach, pecans, and cranberries in the dressing and serve immediately.

Roasted Potatoes

Servings: 20
Cooking Time: 30 Minutes

Ingredients:
- 2lb (1kg) fingerling potatoes, halved
- 1 tbsp chopped fresh cilantro
- 1 tbsp chopped fresh basil
- 1 tbsp chopped scallions, plus more to garnish
- 3 poblano peppers, diced
- 1/2 cup olive oil
- 1/2 cup white vinegar
- 3 garlic cloves, minced
- kosher salt and freshly ground black pepper
- 1 cup crumbled queso fresco

Directions:
1. Preheat the grill to 425°F (218°C) using indirect heat with a standard grate installed. In a dutch oven or a disposable aluminum baking dish, combine potatoes, cilantro, basil, scallions, peppers, oil, vinegar, and garlic. Toss well to ensure potatoes are coated in oil and seasonings. Place the dutch oven on the grate and cook until potatoes are fork tender, about 30 minutes.
2. Remove the dutch oven from the grill, season with salt and pepper to taste, and top with the queso fresco and more sliced scallions. Serve immediately.

Burnt End Baked Beans

Servings: 6
Cooking Time: 30 Minutes

Ingredients:
- 8 oz bacon, finely diced
- 2 cups "burnt ends" from smoked brisket, finely chopped
- 1/2 cup onion, minced
- 2 cloves garlic, minced
- 1 cup favorite barbecue sauce (we like the Classic Texas Barbecue Sauce)
- 1 cup chicken broth
- 1/4 cup brown sugar
- 2 Tablespoons ketchup
- 1 Tablespoon brown mustard
- 2 (15 oz) cans pinto beans, drained and rinsed

Directions:
1. Preheat the grill to 350°F using direct heat with a cast iron grate installed with the dutch oven on the grid.
2. Add the bacon to the dutch oven and cook until crisp.
3. Add onion and garlic and cook 1 minute more.
4. Add remaining ingredients, stir to combine.
5. Cover and lower the dome for 1 hour. Serve hot.

www.ingramcontent.com/pod-product-compliance
Lightning Source LLC
Chambersburg PA
CBHW082042200426
43209CB00053B/1363